Years
in the
Garden

Essays by

Jeanette Stokes

Foreword by Mary E. Hunt

The Resource Center for Women
& Ministry in the South, Inc.

Durham, North Carolina

"Sometimes I Wish" © 1974 Carole Etzler, from her songbook "Take Up the Song".
Reprinted by permission of the author.
"Now Is the Time" © 1977 Carole Etzler, from her tape "Womanriver Flowing On".
Reprinted by permission of the author.
Both are available from her at 1180 VT Route 22A, Bridport, VT 05734.

"Foolish Notion," by Holly Near © 1981 Herford Music, is on the historical collection
Still We Sing: The Outspoken Collection, available in stores and at www.hollynear.com.
Reprinted by permission of the author.

"The first and the last hope of this work," Susan Virginia Hull. Reprinted by permission
of the author.

Scripture quotations are from the Revised Standard Version of the Bible, copyright ©
1946, 1952, and 1971 by the Division of Christian Education of the National Council
of the Churches of Christ in the U.S.A. Used by permission. All rights reserved.

Library of Congress Control Number: 2002093218

ISBN 0-9722035-0-8

First Edition, 2002
10 9 8 7 6 5 4 3 2 1

Copies of this book may be ordered from:
The Resource Center for Women and Ministry in the South, Inc.
1202 Watts Street
Durham, North Carolina 27701
919-683-1236
rcwmsnc@aol.com

Contents

For the women
who nurtured my work
and
encouraged my writing,
especially
Helen Crotwell,
Katherine Fulton, and
Catherine Snyder.

Foreword

Jeanette Stokes has created the genre of feminist inspirational writing. Quite simply, no one does it better. This collection is a welcome compilation that long-time readers will savor and new readers will find a delightful introduction. For all of us, it is a synthetic glimpse into the mind and heart of a savvy woman who is committed to social justice and to living well in the meanwhile. I admire it.

In general, I loathe inspirational writing. It is so syrupy and amorphous as to leave a distasteful residue on the soul. Yet I await every issue of *South of the Garden* eagerly, anxious to know what Jeanette has seen or experienced, what issue has captured her attention and found its way to her powerful pen. I stop whatever I am doing and read her—that marvelous compact style, each piece just long enough to get the point across without any fluff.

Her feminist perspective assures that the essays are predicated on a preferential option for women and dependent children. I can be sure that they are infused with an anti-racist perspective, a critique of capitalism, an assumption of sexual equality and a commitment to social change. This is not "miso soup for the soul," but a hearty helping of healthy, smart ideas. Oh, to sell it at every airport and bookstore in display racks. What a different world we could create!

Jeanette and I met twenty-five years ago at Grailville, a women's community and conference center in Ohio, when we were seminary students. This life-changing feminist theological summer program gave our generation of theologically trained women enough confidence to create new ideas and not simply react cogently to outmoded ones. The experience jump-started our entrepreneurial instincts, not to build empires, but to create more spaces where more people could create more ideas.

Jeanette founded the Resource Center for Women and Ministry in the South in 1977. After more than a decade she tried to leave, but found it would not leave her. So she has made a life for herself, not a lifestyle, but a full, rich life on which she reflects with critical acumen. These essays are testimony to that life and hints of what is to come.

Jeanette's is a woman's life, with all the complexities involved. From her early ministry when she was twenty-something to her seasoned approach now at fifty, she brings a creativity that will not quit. Jeanette engages faithfully in writing, painting, social activism, and living with integrity.

I like her life choice, her unique ministry, as much as I enjoy her writing. She uses her talents and privilege for the common good. There is no higher calling. She keeps plugging away at, indeed living, the contradictions. She makes careful sense and finds meaning where others have sought simple certainties. I always learn from her.

These essays chronicle those years with a "body and soul" approach that pairs local color with global insight. It is spirituality rooted in daily life, the real stuff of gardens and love, heartbreak and friends, colors and textures, protests and farmers' markets. What she writes is not confessional or memoir per se, but a deeper, more distilled version of important issues we all confront. Those of us without her keen eyes appreciate her healthy dose of detail.

She is never self-indulgent. She never reveals more than this reader wants to know. Rather, she says enough to make the point and leaves the rest in her heart where, in my humble opinion, it belongs. This is a delicate balance to achieve when feminist theologians seek to base their work on experience. The temptation to overwhelm the reader with unwarranted detail is one Jeanette models how to avoid.

Still, we know where she comes from: a southern, white, Presbyterian feminist, daughter of a doctor who died when she was young, part of an extended clan that gives her identity, if sometimes it also gives her fits. We know where she lives. I can picture the house and its furnishings though I have never been there. I can see her studio in my mind's eye. I can taste a cup of tea at her office though I have yet to step a foot in it. Jeanette paints with words.

I love her prose. It is spare and elegant. The words carry images far richer than their letters in combination ought to evoke. That is the artist writing, the one who can as easily pick up a brush. Her musings on death are destined to be classics. She takes on that subject about which there is no certainty, and offers a reflection helpful for many who grieve. I love her descriptions of ordinary things, like the "gently sanding process of time," or her own "pointy chin." I can see her strolling to market with her basket and straw hat as easily as I can see her fired up at a presbytery meeting because some people persist in their narrow-minded ways.

Every time I read Jeanette—whether on nature, politics, diversity, whether in sermon format, report or reflection—I come away with a greater sense of clarity and commitment. Such feminist inspiration is hard to find. Now, thanks to this collection, it is at our fingertips for frequent dipping into and widespread sharing. My gratitude abounds, and I am greedy for more.

Mary E. Hunt
Co-Founder and Co-Director, WATER
(Women's Alliance for Theology, Ethics
     and Ritual)
Silver Spring, Maryland

Preface

Shortly after I organized the Resource Center for Women and Ministry in the South, Inc., in 1977, I decided it needed a newsletter. RCWMS was supposed to provide resources and programs on women, ministry, social justice, and spirituality. A newsletter seemed like the best way to begin. I had the good fortune of knowing a first-rate graphic designer, Matilda Kirby-Smith, who created the format we still use and *South of the Garden* was born. The women's movement was in full swing and my first interest was in providing a calendar of events. Listing conferences, workshops, and other events only took up one of the four pages of the newsletter. To fill up the space, I begged articles from friends and wrote the rest myself.

As time went by, I grew to dread and love the writing. I was constantly changing the number of issues per volume. If I said there would be six, there were four or five, because I could not make my own deadlines. Eventually a rhythm emerged of four issues a year. Looking back, it matters little that the intervals between issues were irregular. The joy is that they made it off the press.

I don't actually know when I began to think of myself as a writer. Like Annie Lamott, I have to convince myself of the fact over and over. Evidence helps. I write, so I must be a writer. It occurred to me to gather my essays into a book when I burned out and left my job as the Executive Director of RCWMS in 1995. I planned to create a book that year. That was seven years ago.

This book is dedicated to the women without whom it never would have seen the light of day. The first three who stand out are Helen Crotwell, Katherine Fulton, and Catherine Snyder. Helen was a mentor and friend when I was in seminary. In my early efforts to make space for feminist concerns in religion and in the world, she stood beside me and kept on saying, "Though no one may ever thank you for what you are doing, keep doing it." Her voice has whispered in my ear all through the last twenty-five years. Helen, thank you for being the mother of this work.

Katherine Fulton was a newspaper editor when I lived with her in the 1980s. She helped me switch from a typewriter to a computer and helped me change from being a newsletter editor to being a writer. She dragged stories out of me for her newspaper, *The Independent*. She edited me within an inch of my life. I could have had no finer teacher.

Catherine Snyder saved every copy of *South of the Garden* she ever received, told me over and over how much they meant to her, and wrote me every time she shared one of the essays with a friend. She has never flagged in her support. Catherine, I finally got the collection between two covers. This is for you.

There are so many who have shaped me. My grandmother, May Files Wilkirson, who tied the strings of my heart to the ancestors. My mother, Mary Jeanette Wilkirson Stokes Boswell, who fed my creativity and imagination without needing to understand it. My best-friend-since-I-was-three-years-old, Sally Patton, who has been dragging herself away from her books for almost fifty years to play with me. The woman who encouraged me to try anything I wanted to in the Math Department at Smith College, Alice Dickinson. The woman who convinced me I could invent my work, Janet Kalven. They must be the reason I was able to make up a nonprofit organization twenty-five years ago and keep fooling with it all this time.

These essays would never have been written had it not been for all the women and men who participated in the programs of the Resource Center for Women and Ministry in the South and subscribed to *South of the Garden*. These pages are for all of you. I hope you find some of your stories or history in them.

There are so many who helped to shape this book. Nancy Rosebaugh has been proofreading my essays for as long as I can remember. She began when we were still in seminary. I don't spell well, an important detail in the life of a person who is in love with language. I thought I wasn't good with words because I couldn't spell them all properly. Nancy never once tried to make me feel like an idiot for the mistakes I made.

Margie Hattori read and reread the manuscript until she could recite portions of it. She helped me shape many of the later essays in the book. She is the best at helping me figure out what I'm really trying to say. If you find errors in the text, don't blame Nancy or Margie; I'm sure I was the last one to have my hands on it.

Mary Margaret Wade, Molly Renda, and Michael Brondoli, all professionals in book publishing and design, were generous, patient, and kind in sharing their knowledge and good judgment. I had this crazy idea I'd design the book myself. Mary Margaret came by once a week for months to have a look and make suggestions. Molly answered questions from France where she was in the spring of 2002. Michael offered useful comments on my fledgling efforts to arrange words on the page and helped me find a printer. Thank you, kind friends.

Then there are the generous souls who read through the manuscript. I had twenty-five years of essays, way too many for a book. I needed help in cutting the number down. To leave out any felt like abandoning a child. Mary Jo Cartledge-Hayes, Galia Goodman, Claudia Horwitz, Amy Kellum, Lucy Oliver, Emily Seelbinder, Carter Shelley, and Catherine Snyder read one or more versions of the manuscript.

The essays are finally becoming a book *this* year in honor of the twenty-fifth anniversary of the founding of the Resource Center for Women and Ministry in the South.

In the seven years it has taken to make these essays into a book, there have been many who have offered their suggestions and support. The first challenge was deciding whether to arrange them by topics or by dates. No one could come up with a topical system, so chronology won out. I rather like them in the order in which they were written. They seem to tell a story that way.

Jeanette Stokes
Durham, North Carolina
Summer Solstice 2002

Advent

I would like to share a few images that come to mind when I think of Advent, images of expectation and waiting.

A close friend once went on a long trip. I began to anticipate her return on the very day she left. At first I really missed her. After a while, I came to accept her absence, and the waiting became less intense. Then came the message that she was coming home. My waiting once again was filled with expectation. I could not just sit and twiddle my thumbs. There were friends to call and plans to make. It was just like waiting for Christmas.

Imagine how Mary must have felt. What do you do for nine months while you are pregnant with God? To whom do you talk? Who could possibly understand?

I asked a friend who is expecting a baby at Christmas time what she did when she found out she was pregnant. She said that after the shock wore off, she called a friend who was four or five months along in a pregnancy. She wanted to talk with someone who could understand what she was feeling.

In Luke 1:39–49 we read that an angel appeared to Mary, told her that her relative Elizabeth was also with child. Mary went to her. Imagine the comfort and support the two women might have been to one another. Remember Elizabeth was an old woman, and Mary had no husband. They shared their wonder and their expectation. God placed the miracle of life in each of these female bodies, and God gave them each other as comfort and friend.

Elizabeth might have said, "Be careful. You are carrying God. You must not take any chances. Don't trip, Mary, and don't go on any long donkey rides." How fragile Mary seems, the mother of our savior. She could not have been as delicate as we sometimes picture her, but the awesomeness of her task makes her seem quite vulnerable.

None of you is pregnant with Jesus, and yet, I want to say, "Be careful, you are carrying God." God has entrusted us with the work of the kingdom, just as God entrusted the savior to a young woman's body. God has filled each of us with possibility and given us the responsibility for the care of creation and of one another.

We wait for Christmas, for the coming of the Christ child. As we wait with Mary for the birth of our Lord, let us join in another kind of pregnancy. All of creation is pregnant and groans with pain like the pain of childbirth. Who will be the midwives at the birth of God's new creation? What an impossible task it seems to give birth to the kingdom in this world.

We are not alone. God is with us as we wait expectantly for the birth of a new creation. God gives us one another that we might wait and prepare together.

Volume 2, Number 2, November–December 1979

Women, Faith, & Public Policy

After they had all left and returned to their homes, I tried to figure out what it was that had happened in the short while we spent together.

A year ago the Resource Center for Women and Ministry in the South and the United Church of Christ (UCC) Southern Conference Task Force on Women received a UCC Women's Leadership grant for a conference on Women, Faith, and Public Policy.

For the past six months an ecumenical committee and I have worked together to plan the conference. On April 11 and 12, 1980, sixty participants and resource people spent twenty-four hours together at New Garden Friends Meeting in Greensboro. We, mostly women, came from cities throughout North Carolina and from New York, Atlanta, and Washington, D.C. We were Baptist, Episcopalian, United Church of Christ, Presbyterian, United Methodist, Roman Catholic, and Jewish. We were politicians, theologians, leaders, teachers, ordained ministers, and denominational bureaucrats.

We sang with Carole Etzler, feminist musician from Atlanta; moved with Dot Borden, liturgical dancer from Durham; and worshipped together. We ate wonderful food on tables bedecked with flowers we brought from our gardens.

We talked about how our faith influences our politics, where we get our support, and why we keep working on public policy issues. We shared resources, gave one another support and encouragement, and enlarged our networks. We had workshops on the ERA, grassroots political organizing, and organizing in denominations around women's issues.

After it was all over and I had put Carole Etzler on a plane back to Atlanta, it occurred to me what it was that had happened in the night and day we spent together.

It was church.

We were the people of God, gathered to be challenged and strengthened and dispersed to do God's work.

Volume 2, Number 5, April 1980

God & the Goddess

The three women reminded me of the prophet, the priest, and the rabbi as they sat before us robed in royal purple arguing about the nature of the true religion. Though they said their color coordination was an accident, they function quite literally as leaders of an ever-expanding movement of women who are claiming their own space in spiritual history.

Rosemary Radford Ruether, the one I call the prophet, is a Roman Catholic scholar who has written about the interconnections among various forms of oppression: racism, sexism, anti-Semitism, and the subjugation of the earth.

Carol Christ is a priestess for the women's spirituality movement. Her anthology, *Womanspirit Rising* (Harper & Row, 1979), illustrates the wide variety of ideas being generated by women of spirit today. Her own preference is for a religion that reclaims the Goddess, as she is known through ancient sources and traditions.

Naomi Goldenberg told us that her true vocation was to be a rabbi, but since that was difficult for an atheist feminist in her tradition, she has chosen to be a secular rabbi. She is the author of *Changing of the Gods: Feminism and the End of Traditional Religions* (Beacon, 1979).

These were the panelists in a session on "Women and Religion" at the National Women's Studies Association Conference this year. They do not agree about the task of women in religion today and shared their disagreement in a lively, if not heated, way. The discussion at this session was precipitated by an article in the December 10, 1979, issue of *Christianity and Crisis* by Rosemary Ruether entitled, "A Religion for Women: Sources and Strategies."

Goldenberg rejects biblical religions as hopelessly patriarchal and irredeemable. For her, working on those traditions is just so much wasted energy. Ruether claims that those who work in the Goddess/womanspirit movement are doing so on the basis of shaky scholarship and a somewhat made-up history.

Ruether says that just as Goldenberg finds usable portions of Freud and Jung, she finds liberating insights in the Bible. Goldenberg says that the Wiccan (to do with witches) tradition is no more made up than the Christian tradition.

The argument will go on. I suggest you read the books and articles referred to above. In the meantime, I will offer a few personal reflections.

Ruether's article in *Christianity and Crisis* keeps me from totally abandoning a biblical faith at times when I find it to be overwhelmingly patriarchal. The "usable pieces" of which she speaks are enough to make me want to hang on.

Even if the Bible is thoroughly sexist, that does not change the fact that it is the basis for much of the religion we find in western culture. One can say that the South is irredeemably racist and sexist, but that does nothing to help those of us who are Southerners. I need help, women from biblical traditions need help, in finding our way into, out of, or around our traditions.

The fight may be counterproductive. Ruether put it nicely when she said that for women in traditional religions to communicate with the womanspirit women, we must see that Christianity and Judaism are not the only paths to God; and for the womanspirit women to communicate with traditional women, they must give up some of their hatred of and aversion to the Fathers of the faith.

What we need is to encourage women to find meaningful connections between experience and faith rather than to argue about which way is *the way.*

Volume 2, Number 6, June 1980

Waiting for Justice

For weeks and weeks, Greensboro waited for the verdict in the Nazi-Klan trial. We waited as the jury was selected. We waited as the newspaper reported the tedious details of the evidence. We waited for the jury to arrive at a decision. In the late afternoon on Tuesday, November 17, 1980, the verdict was announced. We were horrified.

I was in my office that afternoon when the news reached me. I had not even allowed myself to imagine that all of the defendants might get off. My immediate reaction was to want to go home and lock the door. I was afraid. Afraid of violence, afraid that justice had gone to sleep and would never be roused again, afraid that none of us would have anything to say in the face of what felt like the failure of ourselves, our city, our courts, our justice.

I went home, ate dinner, and listened to radio and TV news at the same time. There seemed to be no immediate threat of violence. It was raining.

At about 7:30 p.m. I went out again, to a meeting of the Guilford County Women's Political Caucus, being held at the Greensboro YWCA. There I saw the women with whom I had worked for the ERA for the past few years. Only two weeks before, our hopes for ratification had been all but dashed by the election of an unexpectedly conservative North Carolina legislature.

I sat quietly on the floor and made notes to myself on a pad. "I am burned out," I wrote. "I am completely burned out." As I sat there waiting, waiting for healing, waiting for hope, waiting for justice to come back from wherever it had gone, I saw Dorothy Bardolph.

Dorothy is a retired college professor. She and I worked together on McNeill Smith's campaign for the United States Senate. We lost that one. We worked to save the little house next to the YMCA that was in danger of being torn down for a parking lot. We worked to get a ward system in the city and failed by a very close margin. We worked and got Dorothy elected to the city council. I thought to myself, "Dorothy Bardolph has been working for justice for more years than I have been alive. Who am I to be tired?"

I saw Carolyn Allen, President of the North Carolina League of Women Voters, who takes on issue after issue and never seems to give out or give up.

I looked around and I remembered that justice is not something that comes once and for all. The kingdom is never fully revealed. It is here, and it is coming. I looked around and saw those women who have been preparing a way for justice, preparing a way for the kingdom, preparing a way for the dignity of all persons for years and years.

I looked around and thought of the words to "Sometimes I Wish" by Carole Etzler:

> *Sometimes I wish my eyes hadn't been opened,*
> *Sometimes I wish I could no longer see*
> *All of the pain and the hurt and the longing*
> *Of my sisters and me as we try to be free.*

The song goes on to say,

> *Sometimes I wish my eyes hadn't been opened,*
> *But now that they have, I'm determined to see*
> *That somehow my sisters and I will be one day*
> *The free people we were created to be.*

There is more to waiting than just sitting there. Justice does not just happen. Our church, our community, and our society are what we make of them. We are not a powerless people, and we must not give up.

Volume 3, Number 2, December 1980

Work & the Woman Minister

Carole Etzler passed through Greensboro in an eighteen-foot yellow Hertz truck the week before Thanksgiving. She was moving her belongings from Atlanta to Vermont. On the spur of the moment, I decided to ride along, but not without some agonizing over work time I would miss. I knew the break would be good for me, but I feared feeling irresponsible.

We visited friends along the way, read, sang, and talked of a God who has an interdependent relationship with creation. I spent Thanksgiving in Boston and contacted people who work on projects and issues related to my work. It was renewing and invigorating and included enough work to keep me from feeling too guilty.

"Work?" Maynard G. Krebs used to shriek on the Dobie Gillis Show. Work is both friend and foe. Women in ministry have two perpetual problems with work. The first is finding work. The second is not letting the work kill us.

Ministers think it acceptable to work 60–70 hours a week. I think it is terrible, even unethical. Large corporations are learning that their executives are more productive if they work no more than 40–50 hours a week. The church has not caught on yet. We are still tempted by a "more is better" approach to work.

Some friends of mine spent all last year trying to teach me the difference between work and play. I used to think that when work did not hurt, it was play. *Wrong*. Work is still work even when it does not hurt.

An understanding of Sabbath I learned at Grailville is helpful here. On the Sabbath, people are to enjoy God's creation instead of trying to improve on it. The other six days of the week, we can try to make the world a better place for everyone to live. Some people work so hard trying to make the world a better place for everyone to live that they have no life of their own and hardly ever get to enjoy creation.

When people ask me what Carole Etzler is doing now, I say, "She does not have a job, she is having a life." (She is also writing a book and doing music.) If you can't tell the difference between work and play, between improving creation and enjoying it, you need help. A small child may be able to assist you.

We work too hard for many reasons. Women, anxious to prove that we can make it in the male world of work, may get caught in working all the time. One woman says she works so she won't have time to think about her life. Many of us work on things to which we are strongly committed. Still, we must ask, "How much is enough?" and "Are more hours of work really the answer?"

Any woman who enters the male world of work is almost guaranteed to overwork. The male workday is designed for the worker who has someone at home to feed, clothe, and love him. So one answer would be to change the system.

Rosemary Ruether's article, "Toward New Solutions: Working Women and the Male Workday" (*Christianity & Crisis*, February 7, 1977), suggests that twenty-five hours might be an adequate workweek, providing a livable wage and time for a life.

Overwork, for whatever reason, can cause burnout, illness, stress, and can make you very hard to live with. Two suggestions for those of you who still insist on trying to make it in the work world as we now know it: 1) Aim for minimum input and maximum output; 2) Give out of your overflow.

Diane Tennis once suggested that women were guilty of maximum input for minimum output. I think my mother had figured out this principle when she said she was not going to bake any more cookies for school fundraisers but would be glad to contribute what she would have spent on ingredients. Look at your Committee on Women's Concerns, or ERA fundraiser, and ask how they measure up to the minimum input/maximum output rule.

In Sally Gearheart's *The Wanderground* (Persephone, 1979), one woman pours affection out to another and reminds herself, "If I do not give from my overflow, then what I give is poison." There will be times when we have to reach down to the bottom of our well of strength and dredge up the last drop. If we live and work that way every day, we won't live or work very long.

Give what you know to give. Do what is easy for you. Use your talents, but not all the time. And if Carole Etzler ever passes by in a yellow truck, hitch a ride.

Note: Carole Etzler left a media job at the Presbyterian Church, U.S. headquarters in Atlanta to move to Vermont. Diane Tennis was the Presbyterian Church, U.S. staff person responsible for clergywomen.

Volume 4, Number 2, December 1981

Women Doing Theology

The word "theology" comes from two Greek words: "theos" meaning God, and "logos" meaning word. Theology, then, is words about God.

We all have words to say about God, but some of us think that people who have studied theology in institutions of higher education have a corner on the truth about God. Professional theologians may be helpful to us, but they certainly are not the only people who can speak with authority or whose visions are reliable. The theological profession may, in fact, function in such a way as to discourage others from saying their own words about God.

I spent several weeks in the summer of 1976 with women in the Seminary Quarter at Grailville (a Catholic women's educational center in Ohio) trying to find new ways to talk about God, new ways to do theology. Nelle Morton, a wise woman who has helped generations of women find their own words to say about God, was with us for part of that time. She is the one who says that by listening to one another women hear one another into being.

Nelle often spoke about "women doing theology," so I asked her when women's words were theology and when they were just talk. She said that women's words are theology when women speak to one another out of the depths of their beings about the things they care most about.

Ever since that summer at Grailville, I have searched and longed for places to gather with women and to do theology as Nelle describes it. The Resource Center for Women and Ministry in the South was created in an effort to discover, invent, and publicize opportunities for women to do theology together. I periodically satisfy my longing at a workshop, a professional meeting, or with a group of friends.

Doing theology, or theologizing as we sometimes call it, can happen spontaneously, or it can be encouraged by organized gatherings. The calendar in this issue of *South of the Garden* is filled with opportunities for women to reflect, to theologize, and to share experiences. I hope that you will be able to take advantage of some of them.

The men? Oh, they can and do theologize, and we can do theology together. My concern at this point in history, though, is that women add the words that grow out of our particular experiences to a stream of theological language that has been determined largely by men.

Note: Nelle Morton, author of The Journey is Home *(Beacon, 1985), was for many years on the faculty of the Theological School of Drew University.*

Volume 4, Number 3, March 1982

Failure is Impossible

Now is the time for all good women
To stand up and say who we will be.
Now is the time for all good women
To stand up and fight, to start claiming the right,
The right to be free.

We've waited so long we've half forgotten
Our mothers who fought, who struggled before.
We've waited so long we've half forgotten
But we're seizing our fate, we're not gonna wait
Ten thousand years more.
                    —Carole Etzler, "Now is the Time"

Now is the time.

On May 1, 1982, the green and white buttons distributed by NOW for the ERA countdown campaign will read "2." Just two more months until the June 30 deadline for ratification of the Equal Rights Amendment.

A miracle occurred in the North Carolina General Assembly in April, a well-planned miracle. Condemned to a silent death by a "gentlemen's agreement" not to consider the bill, the ERA had slept for the months of the Fall/Winter recess. But on April 5, the stone was rolled away. On the last day it was to meet, a legislative study commission voted to include an ERA ratification bill in its report to be presented when the legislature reconvenes June 2.

"It's happening, it's happening," a friend called to say on the morning of April 5. Sure enough, when I picked up the paper the next morning, what I had known as a secret plan since July had finally occurred. Some political finesse had accomplished what hundreds of demonstrators and thousands of letters might never have wrought.

We may not succeed, but at least we will get to try again.

Susan B. Anthony said, "Failure is impossible." For some time now I have meditated on that saying. What do you mean, failure is impossible? Of course it is possible. Some days it even seems probable. Then, one day last winter, it "clicked." Of course failure is impossible! Should June 30 arrive without ratification by the necessary thirty-eight states, the current attempt at passage will fail. But for us, the women of this state who have given our time, energy, money, youth, and love to this cause, there will be no failure.

We have been converted. We have come to see the world in a new way. We have gained skills and confidence. We cannot go back.

I watched an ERA documentary on PBS last night called, "Who Will Protect the Family?" It told the story of the 1979 and 1981 attempts at ratification in North Carolina. It told the story, all right, but it failed to capture the life, the passion, the tears, and the faith of the women and men who have fought this battle for the last ten years.

In the past, we have fought for our children and for our loved ones. We have fought for justice and for decency. But what continues to fuel our passion and sustain our efforts in this struggle is that we are fighting for ourselves. In this struggle for justice and equity, we have won the greatest prize, our own dignity, our own vision of the world, our own lives.

We take our newly found skills and pride back into our homes, back into our jobs, out into campaigns for elective office, and into battles for other legislation. The things we return to and the new things we try are changed just as we were, slowly, surely.

In the wake of this metamorphosis, failure is a name by which we will never again call ourselves.

Volume 4, Number 4, May 1982

Revenge

The Equal Rights Amendment (ERA) was defeated, again, in the North Carolina Senate on June 4, 1982. I witnessed the four successive votes that tabled the amendment and made reconsideration virtually impossible.

The votes were followed by a moment of stunned silence. Then a few people in the gallery started chanting, "Greene, Greene, Greene," the name of the Lt. Governor who chairs the Senate and is anti-ERA. Mr. Greene rapped his gavel and ordered that the gallery be cleared. There was silence again.

Then it erupted. *Rage*. The spirit that wants justice broke through. "ERA won't go away. ERA won't go away." Again and again. The halls of the legislature rang with our anger and our protest. The message was clear: "We will be back, and we will have our rights."

The chanting went on for a full ten minutes while we filed out of the gallery, into the lobby, and finally out to the front of the building. It felt so good to scream. Those jerks!

One definition of revenge is "an opportunity for getting satisfaction." Screaming was personally satisfying but not very effective.

I put a bumper sticker on my car as part of my revenge: "Adam was a rough draft." I also resorted to a vacation, long walks, cleaning out closets, and sleeping late. Often since June 4, I have thought of the saying that the best revenge is living well.

Some unidentified person's revenge was to send chicken manure to the twenty-seven senators who voted against the ERA. Some thought the gesture showed bad taste. I rather liked it.

Ann Lewis of the Democratic National Committee offers another version of revenge, "The only way to change policy is by changing policymakers." By the time elections are over, it is too late to influence legislators.

My plea is that people of faith involve themselves in the political process. Work for the candidates of your choice. Better yet, run for office yourself. The ERA battle has sent some fine women out into the political fray, women such as Bett Hargrave, candidate for county commissioner in Davidson County, North Carolina; Winnie Wood in eastern North Carolina, who has challenged an anti-ERA senator in the primary; and Betty J. Pierce who filed for a state judgeship.

We might even revive the old Congregational tradition of election eve sermons endorsing candidates.

A national campaign to ratify ERA will begin all over again in July when it is likely to be reintroduced in Congress. Until then, send President Reagan postcards prepared by the Religious Committee for ERA that say, "Don't let the fire of equality be snuffed out."

Volume 4, Number 5, July 1982

Women's Spirit Bonding

We were 130 women together for a week in July, gathered for a feminist theological conference at Grailville, a 350-acre farm and retreat center outside Cincinnati, Ohio.

As I remember the conference, called "Women's Spirit Bonding," one notion surfaces again and again: diversity. One of the thirty panelists, Jacqueline Grant of the Interdenominational Center in Atlanta, put it clearly when she said that the only way to create a holistic feminist theology is to take the experiences of lots of diverse women into account. That is exactly what we spent a week trying to do. Women from a variety of ethnic, religious, and cultural backgrounds spoke to one another out of their own unique experiences; they spoke of their deepest concerns.

Experience is the raw material of feminist theology. It is the basis, the context, the source out of which theology grows. Being with a whole bunch of women willing to reflect on the relationship between their own experiences and their understanding of the holy was like water on dry ground for me. I just soaked it up. I felt like my brain had come alive again.

Gathering together at Grailville reminded me of a chapter in Sally Gearhart's *The Wanderground* (Persephone, 1979) called "Gatherstretch." The chapter describes the negotiating process of the hill women, the book's main characters.

At Grailville, we were gathered, and not just gathered together. We were gathered in. We were loved by old friends and new ones, treated to the sights and smells of one of the most comforting places on earth, fed wonderful food, and provided with places to walk, swim, do yoga, and meditate. All day long, women said interesting things.

We were stretched. Encountering diversity can help people grow. It can stretch our imaginations, broaden our understandings. It can also pull and tear at us. Diversity can cause misunderstanding, conflict, and pain.

CONFLICT

Some of the ways we stretch each other were revealed during a session on "Racism, Pluralism, and Bonding." Presentations on racism against blacks, the Hispanic experience, anti-Semitism, and white women and racism only scratched the surface of our differences.

There were many kinds of differences among us. There was lack of understanding for the experience of some, and this was challenged. "You people don't know anything about oppression," railed one white working-class woman. She was not amused that some of the participants considered it an honor to have served time in jail. "I've been to jail, and it wasn't for civil disobedience. It was for shoplifting to get enough money for food."

There were differences within groups. Ada Maria Isasi-Diaz reminded us that no one Hispanic perspective speaks for all Hispanic women. Mexican Americans have a different experience from Cuban Americans. Hispanic people who live in Texas, Florida or New York do not share an identical heritage.

And there was conflict between groups. During the panel on racism, Judith Plaskow, a Jewish theologian, pointed out the history of anti-Semitism against Jews. In the discussion following the panel, Mary Abu-Saba, whose husband is Lebanese, spoke out of the deep pain brought on by the war raging in the Middle East and reminded us that Arabs are Semites too. She warned that the conflict in the Middle East is the one that threatens to blow us up most immediately and that it cannot be ignored. Judith Plaskow bristled and responded with a story about the hatefulness of a PLO woman at the International Women's Conference in Copenhagen.

HEALING

Given such differences, the question becomes: How can the diverse spirits that are women come together and bond in a way that is healing?

The negotiating process of the "gatherstretch" is helpful here. In a "gatherstretch" conflicting women agree to yield, if it comes to that. What is required is not that one yield, but that she be willing to do so. Out of that willingness often comes a solution with which everyone can live. That kind of openness to difference is what an Hispanic woman at Grailville was talking about when she encouraged us to "go out of our minds" to understand the world of people who are different.

What happens to make understanding and even yielding possible? Mary Elizabeth Hunt, a young Catholic theologian who was a panelist at the conference, suggested that it is our own experience that is the bridge to other people. Each of us has a personal experience of racism, sexism, heterosexism, imperialism, or some other incarnation of oppression. From our own lives each of us has a way to understand the oppression of others. Mary Elizabeth spent the past couple of years teaching in Buenos Aires. Her experience as a woman made it easier to understand the oppression of the Argentines.

Finding a bridge does not take all the differences or the pain away. People often look for bonding and healing too soon. Just because a wound has stopped bleeding does not mean that it has healed. Jamie Phelps, a black woman religious from Washington, D.C., warned against "cheap grace," and encouraged us not to lose sight of the differences between us.

Some participants at the conference were surprised at Mary Abu-Saba's words during the closing celebration. She was invited to offer one of seven blessings over the lighting of candles. Hers were the words of the prophets demanding justice. Some thought that because she and Judith Plaskow had been able to laugh together and drink wine together that everything was fine. Everything was not fine. Judith still wanted safety for Israel, and Mary still wanted the Israelis out of Lebanon.

BONDING

Mary and Judith never completely resolved their differences, but they did begin to create a bridge of understanding between them by hearing each other and allowing the other her own way of seeing the world. When women achieve that sort of understanding across diversity, then and only then do we begin to have women's spirit bonding.

Bonding is what happens when we get to know other people and to care about them, to appreciate the things we like about them and the things we don't like, the things that are familiar and the things that we don't understand. Bonding is what happened for a week at Grailville in July.

Bonding does not come easily or quickly, especially for women from different cultures and traditions. But we need to hear one another and to find solutions to our differences other than shooting at one another.

Women's spirit bonding—our survival depends on it. Our vision of the future depends on it. And our theology depends on it. We need the experiences of all the people of the world if we are ever going to figure out what justice looks like and how we are going to live together equitably. We need the voices of diverse women if we are ever going to have a truly feminist theology.

Volume 5, Number 1, September 1982

The Word

If ever there were word-oriented religions, Judaism and Christianity are among them. "And God said, 'Let there be light.'" "In the beginning was the Word." In many Protestant seminaries, students are taught that it takes twenty hours to prepare the right words for Sunday morning.

Feminists are also interested in words. Calling people "men" will not do, we say, because the word "men" does not and never was intended to include women (e.g., "All men are created equal"). Many of us over the age of eighteen also object to the term "girl."

From time to time, scientists and engineers have turned their attention to the word and have invented tools and machines to help us handle words. There must have been some purists who greeted the invention of the fountain pen, the typewriter, or the ballpoint with dread, saying, "Machines don't write, people do." That's right, but I, for one, need all the help I can get. Even an IBM self-correcting Selectric typewriter only takes a little of the pain out of writing. If a friend is kind enough to read something and to offer a few suggestions, my first thought is always that I will have to type the whole thing over.

Never again! A miracle has been wrought by modern science and technology and is due to arrive in my office next week: a word processing computer.

A word processing computer is a computer that will help you with writing and editing but will also compute. They now come in a small size, are called personal computers, and take up as much room as a small TV and typewriter. For good word processing you need several pieces: a central processing unit, a keyboard, a video display screen, a program (software) for word processing, and a printer.

Three weeks ago, I didn't know the difference between a bit and a byte and had never even learned to use the memory on my calculator. Now I can speak computerese with the best of them. Two books by Peter A.

McWilliams, *The Personal Computer Book* (Prelude, 1982) and *The Word Processing Book* (Prelude, 1983), demystified computers for me. I highly recommend them for any beginner.

By the way, you don't have to understand how computers work to be able to use them, just as you don't have to understand aerodynamics to get from Atlanta to Dallas on an airplane. If you've never been very good with machines, don't worry. Using a word processing computer is not much more complicated than an electric typewriter or getting money out of one of those automated bank machines.

Before you get the idea that I have sold out to the machines, let me explain. My enthusiasm began last fall when a friend was kind enough to enter one of my sermons into her word processing system. After a little editing and suggestions for rearrangement, she pushed a few buttons, and the sermon had a whole new shape.

One resourceful friend pointed out that a word processing computer would be cheaper than a secretary. And so it is. $5,000 will get you a whale of a word processing computer, but it wouldn't pay a secretary for long. (Secretaries needn't be alarmed. A machine for that amount of money can't begin to replace you.) You're right, that is a lot of money, but you can do it for less; and think of the long-term return.

Imagine putting the scissors and tape in the drawer with the wrapping paper and forgetting how to "cut and paste." Even if you did not finish a sermon until 2:00 on Sunday morning, it would be all in one piece and typed. You could even leave the sermon in the computer's memory, pull it out at some future date, make a few changes, and use the same sermon again (in a new setting, of course) without retyping it.

Other special features that make personal computers attractive to churches are programs that will help keep up with members, contributions, books, etc. Think what a word processing computer can do for your bulletins. The format would be in the memory; the details could be changed each week.

But you don't have to listen to me rave about computers, go to see one for yourself. Personal computers are sold in retail stores like TVs and radios. Don't expect too much of the salespeople. They may or may not know more than how to make change. Read a few books and magazine articles and find a friend who knows something about computers. Perhaps in a few weeks or months a miracle will come to live in your office, too.

Volume 5, Number 3, January 1983

Inclusive Language

I feel like *Newsweek* said my mother wears army boots. In a recent story about *An Inclusive Language Lectionary: Readings for Year A* (John Knox/Pilgrim/Westminster, 1983), the magazine stated, "Occasionally, the new lectionary sounds like Scripture as translated by the Coneheads."

I was caught off guard by this and other negative reactions to the new lectionary. Since I have waited for such a document for ten years, the critics are the ones who seem like Coneheads to me. Their objections are many and varied. I will address a few.

"If we accept the Holy Bible as the Word of God, then it should remain so, unchanged," objected one man in a letter to the editor of a local newspaper. In other words, no one should tamper with the Bible.

In the first place *An Inclusive Language Lectionary* is not a Bible. It is a lectionary.

A lectionary is a list of scripture lessons to be read and heard in worship services. The idea is to expose worshippers to large portions of the Bible over the course of several years. The new lectionary covers only the first year in a three-year cycle, hence Year A in the lectionary's title.

The National Council of Churches committee that developed the inclusive lectionary used the Revised Standard Version of the Bible and scripture lessons listed in the 1974 Consultation on Church Union Lectionary. Each passage was recast to minimize the male bias reflected in the RSV's language about human beings, about Christ, and about God.

For instance, *Then the Lord God said, "It is not good that the man should be alone, I will make him a helper fit for him." (Gen. 2:18) becomes Then God the Sovereign One said, "It is not good that the human being should be alone; I will make a companion corresponding to the creature."*

For God so loved the world that he gave his only Son, that whoever believes in him should not perish but have eternal life. (John 3:16) becomes *For God so loved the world that God gave God's only Child, that whoever believes in that Child should not perish but have eternal life.*

The new lectionary provides alternative translations. It is completely optional and is offered to the church as a provisional, experimental, and responsible attempt to proclaim the biblical message in an inclusive manner.

As for the charge of tampering with scriptures, we tamper every time we translate. If we left the Bible "unchanged," I dare say few in this country could read it. The Old Testament was written in Hebrew and the New Testament in Greek. To complicate matters, Jesus spoke Aramaic, so all of his words were translated first from Aramaic to Greek by the authors of the New Testament and then from Greek to other languages by translators. Because no language is a perfect match for any other, every translation is an interpretation.

The word of God is not simply the words themselves, but the message of God addressed to God's people. Christians believe that the word of God was made present among us in Jesus Christ. The Bible provides us with an understanding of God, not with a set of magic words.

There is a second category of objection made by people who think inclusive language is just a stupid idea. "I still say 'congressman,' not 'congressperson,'" editorialized one female supporter of the ERA who objects to the new lectionary.

Inclusive language is not a stupid idea. It is a powerful and important concept, even though it results in language some people find jarring. Consider the use of the generic in the English language. The masculine pronoun is used to refer to a member of a group of males and females. Feminists question whether the masculine really includes or was ever intended to include women.

Take the Constitution of the United States, for example. It is no accident that the Constitution says, "all men were created equal." It says, "men." It means "men." "Men" in this case was never intended to mean females. Only subsequent amendments have included women in our founding document.

Another example of the power of the generic is the use of a particular brand name for a whole class of products. Kleenex and Xerox are two examples that have made their way into household usage and are used instead of "tissue" and "photocopier." Some benefit accrues to those two companies by virtue of their brand names being used as the generic. When we say "Xerox," we all know we really mean a photocopier, but ask Canon if they feel included in the word "Xerox." Of course they don't.

The use of the male as the generic in English affords a political benefit to males. A generic can be used by convention, but it never really includes everyone, and was probably never intended to.

Finally, we come to this business about the sex of God. Some who agree that inclusive language is important in reference to people still feel that God ought to be referred to as male.

Some argue that God is really male, in which case I would like for them to verify divine genitalia. When God created human beings, they were created in the image of God, and they were both male and female. If the image of God is both male and female, then we must consider that God may also be male and female.

Other critics concede that God is not really male, but say, "It doesn't bother me that God is presented as male. God is traditionally portrayed as male."

"It doesn't bother me."

It does not bother most people that Arabs are portrayed as thieving, or that Jews are portrayed as stingy, or that blacks are portrayed as slow—in literature, in advertising, in the culture generally. Tradition does not make those portrayals just, right, or acceptable.

Maybe we like simple answers and are afraid to admit that we don't know, never will know, the true nature of God. Perhaps we cling to the notion that God is male because it is familiar. But worshipping a male God is not the answer and is not faithful to God's message to us.

The Bible is very patriarchal. It would be a mistake to try to erase all of the male dominance in the Bible, for it would hide the existence of male-dominated societies of Biblical times. The question is how to use the Bible in the context of worship without leaving out more than half of the worshipping community.

Perhaps it is a good thing that *An Inclusive Language Lectionary* sounds a little awkward to some people. It makes it clear that the writers of scripture often excluded women and that including women in a traditionally male-dominated religion is not a simple matter. Even so, I think saying it sounds like Coneheads is a little harsh.

In the end, critics and enthusiasts alike would have to agree that, regardless of our personal preferences, the English language is changing. From the government's use of "Ms." to the Presbyterian *Book of Order's* reference to the minister as "he or she," language about people is changing.

Language about God is changing, too. It is changing because women and men of faith insist that the motherly as well as the fatherly characteristics of God be worshipped in the presence of the sisterhood and brotherhood of all humankind.

This Christmas join me in singing "God rest ye merry gentle folk" and sharing the good news of peace on earth, good will to all.

Volume 6, Number 1, November–December 1983

Death Row

Twice this year I have found myself standing in front of the North Carolina governor's office the afternoon before a scheduled execution, both times on behalf of James Hutchins.

As I prepared for one vigil, I tried to make a poster but could not decide what to put on it. All of the slogans I thought of reminded me of the signs antiabortion people parade in front of clinics. My confusion was only a symbol of a deeper problem: what to say to people about the death penalty.

I was surprised by lots of people's reactions to James Hutchins' plight. To a group of teenage girls walking past the vigil, it seemed a simple enough proposition: "He killed somebody; he deserves to be killed." Hammurabi developed a similar code of justice almost 4,000 years ago ("an eye for an eye and a tooth for a tooth"), but I thought our moral development had grown beyond that.

I was shocked at otherwise liberal friends' reactions. One said simply that she was in favor of the death penalty. Another said it wasn't very important. After all, it was only one man and he had done some pretty horrible things.

A more reasoned opinion came from a police officer who was keeping the peace at the vigil. I was interested in his opinion, because James Hutchins was convicted of killing three police officers. The officer said he thought more people would give up the death penalty if there were a reliable alternative. He meant life without parole.

I'd go along with that, but there is currently no such provision in North Carolina law. One death penalty opponent mused that if we aren't careful, we could wind up with both the death penalty and life without parole.

So what do people of faith say to folks who don't think the issue is of much importance, who want "an eye for an eye," or who want to blow the bandits away?

First of all, there is no evidence that the death penalty deters anyone from any crime. It does not make any of us safer.

Second, we do not have a perfect system of justice. Even if it were just to kill someone convicted of murder, our system makes mistakes. Innocent people have died in gas chambers and electric chairs. There is no changing the sentence once someone is dead.

Third, our system of justice is not applied equally to everyone. Some people convicted of murder, for instance, are sentenced to death and others are not. Rich people are able to pay for better lawyers than poor people. The race of the killer and the victim influences judges and juries.

Finally, I don't care who the person is or what s/he has done. James Hutchins could be Jack the Ripper. The death penalty is an outrage, no matter who we are talking about. On March 16 the state killed Hutchins in the first North Carolina execution since 1961.

Unfortunately, I expect to take a poster and stand in front of the governor's office again this summer. This time the person whose life will be at stake is a woman.

Velma Barfield, convicted of poisoning her fiancé and sentenced to death in 1978, could be the first woman executed in the United States since the death penalty was reinstated in 1976. Her legal remedies have been all but exhausted. Her best hope is the Honorable James B. Hunt, Governor of North Carolina and a candidate for the United States Senate. He has the power to grant clemency, but did not choose to spare James Hutchins' life. Public pressure is our only chance.

Clemency is especially appropriate in this case for several reasons. First, Velma Barfield had a long history of drug addiction prior to the murder. She needed help. Second, she has had a very good record while in the North Carolina Correctional Center for Women. Many of the officials and inmates at the prison are fond of her. She is good with young inmates who are having problems. She could continue living there as a useful member of the community.

Even if Velma Barfield were not the warm, brave person that she is, people of faith would still need to cry out against the death penalty. Talk to your friends about the issue and join a vigil at the governor's office. For a sign, try words from singer Holly Near's song, *Foolish Notion*:

> *Why do we kill people who are killing people*
> *To show that killing people is wrong?*

Volume 6, Number 4, June 1984

Boycott

The Boston Tea Party, Rosa Parks, the slogan "Don't Sleep with J. P. Stevens," and Nestlé chocolate chips all have one thing in common. They have all been part of a boycott in America.

Boycotts have become a way of life. They have changed my eating habits and made me aware of the size of some of America's conglomerates.

Because of the Nestlé boycott, I gave up making chocolate chip cookies (other chips didn't taste the same). Chocolate chip cookies weren't good for me anyway, even if I had perfected a "crisp-on-the-outside, chewy-on-the-inside" cookie.

I used to love Stouffer's Noodles Romanoff. Stouffer is part of Nestlé, so I gave up Noodles Romanoff. The frozen foods section made me sad. It reminded me of noodles I couldn't have and of unhealthy babies, so I gave up just about everything frozen except green peas and piecrusts.

I could never get anyone in a grocery store to tell me if the iceberg lettuce was Red Coach or not, so I just stopped eating the stuff. I now prefer any other kind of lettuce, and this fall, for the first time, I am growing my own.

After watching the chairman (and he was a man) of the Board of J. P. Stevens insult workers, priests, and nuns on the floor of a stockholder's meeting in Greenville, South Carolina, I can't see a Stevens sheet without thinking of that man. Believe me, I will remember the slogan "Don't Sleep with J. P. Stevens" long after the boycott is over.

There is little I can do as an individual to influence corporate America. I don't buy products from companies I don't like, but most of those companies don't know it. I am willing to join with other people in a boycott because our collective voice is more likely to be heard than mine alone.

I'm also willing to participate because in interrupting my reflex to buy certain things, I remind myself of larger issues that need attention. It's sort of like fasting. It may not help the people who hurt, but it does remind us that we need to do something about their hurt.

Some boycotts end successfully. An agreement was reached between the International Nestlé Boycott Committee and Nestlé on January 25, 1984. An international infant formula code has been established to protect children in developing countries from hazards related to inappropriate marketing of infant formula.

The boycott is over, but the work is not done. After-boycott work includes verifying compliance with the new code, seeking compliance in developed countries, and linking the practices of other multinational corporations to this agreement.

Other boycotts continue. Cesar Chavez and the United Farm Workers, AFL-CIO have called for a renewal of the international boycott of non-union California table grapes according to Joan Papert Preiss, chairperson of the North Carolina volunteer support group, Triangle Friends of the United Farm Workers.

According to Chavez, "The table grape industry was targeted because wages, benefits, and working conditions in the vineyards lag far behind other industries." Grape workers' buying power has dropped since 1977 while growers' income has increased substantially.

In addition, Chavez charged that California labor law has been undermined since the election of Governor Deukmejian and that the farm workers are not receiving the rights and protections that the law was designed to provide.

In the Midwest, farm workers, under the leadership of the Farm Labor Organizing Committee (FLOC), have been on strike since 1978 in tomato fields contracted to the Campbell Soup Company. A boycott of Campbell products began in 1979 to protest child labor, sub-minimum wages, inhumane housing and pesticide poisonings. Farm workers want and need a contract with the Campbell Company to end these conditions. The strike and boycott will continue until Campbell agrees to negotiate with farm workers and the growers. For six years, Campbell has refused to listen to farm workers, but they may listen to the public. You can support the people who feed this country by supporting the boycott.

Note: FLOC, the growers, and Campbell eventually negotiated a three-way agreement. Organizers believe the boycott helped bring about the agreement.

Volume 7, Number 1, October 1984

Spirituality

I do encourage people to be bodacious enough to invent their own lives everyday. Otherwise, somebody will invent it for you.

—Maya Angelou

I woke up on Easter morning depressed. It was a glorious day, and every cell in my body longed for a community with which to celebrate freedom from winter, from slavery, and from death.

As a campus minister, I have no Sunday congregation, and what really feels like my "community" is scattered in and out of a variety of churches. So I surveyed my options. I could attend the big church with wonderful music and a theology I find objectionable. Or the smaller church where one of my colleagues struggles to enliven the congregation. Or the Unitarian Church with a great minister and congregation but no ritual.

Finally I selected the Episcopal Student Center at the University of North Carolina at Greensboro, where I have been meeting with a small group on inclusive language and liturgy. I knew I would find a few friends, and, as it turned out, I also found a splendid trumpeter.

My sadness on Easter morning put me in touch with a larger question. Can a feminist feel spiritually at home anywhere?

Looking for a spiritual community where one can feel at home is like looking for a lover. It is seeking a community where our images of God and our experiences of the holy will be welcomed. In a sexual relationship, we expect to bring our whole selves. Why then would we expect women to participate in spiritual relationships to which we can only bring part of ourselves?

Spirituality and sexuality are connected. Both involve sharing. Both involve choice. We need the freedom to reinvent both of them for ourselves instead of being forced to use someone else's form.

Mary Abu-Saba, a friend and a therapist, teaches people to say, "My sexuality is for me." It is not for someone else. If I choose to share it with someone else, it is my choice. That is a far cry from the old definition of a wife's body being for her husband.

Owning one's sexuality is still problematic, even for liberated women today. Men, indoctrinated by patriarchal culture, have narrowed the definition of "sex" to suit their own tastes. There may be activities before and after, but everyone knows when "it" is happening.

My spirituality is also for me. Maya Angelou is right. If we don't make it up for ourselves, someone else will make it up for us. Not making it up for myself is what made me sad on Easter morning. Next Easter will be different.

To get ready, I'll read "Sexuality, Love, and Justice" in Carter Heyward's *Our Passion for Justice* (Pilgrim, 1984) and Diann Neu's *Women Church Celebrations: Feminist Liturgies for the Lenten Season* (WATERworks, 1985).

Volume 7, Number 4, March–April 1985

Turning Fifty

Rituals are a part of our everyday lives: reading the newspaper, checking the weather, waiting for the mail to come, or talking with a family member at the end of the day. Rituals can also mark the extraordinary events in our lives: the birth of a child, the death of a loved one, a birthday, marriage, anniversary, or divorce.

Creating the right ritual for the right occasion is not always easy. *South of the Garden* shares rituals with its readers from time to time. Here is a description of one for a friend who turned fifty years of age.

On the Ides of March, Mary K. Wakeman invited thirty of her friends to help celebrate her fiftieth birthday. She asked some people to bring food and others of us to create a ritual for the occasion.

Allan Troxler, a friend who helped with the plan, suggested that a ritual should start from the inside. We thought about what reminded us of Mary K. and came up with weaving and words, two things we associate with this teacher of religion and weaver of tapestries.

We asked people coming to the party to bring something they could weave into a large tapestry. After dinner we read a poem about weaving, noted that Mary K. is part of the fabric of our lives as we are part of hers, and began the weaving.

A two-by-four-foot "loom" was constructed by lashing some brightly colored poles together and warping it with yarn. People wove in bits of fabric, feathers, string, flowers, ribbon, yarn, the rip-off edges of computer paper, and violin strings. We were all quite pleased with ourselves at having created something interesting. Each person offered a few words about the threads they had added to the weaving.

Mary K. is a teacher and writer, so we asked the guests to bring words they had heard her say. We wanted Mary K. to know that her words were not lost in the world but live on in her friends. We shared words we had heard her say and left them on slips of paper for her to read again.

As a closing, everyone over fifty gathered around Mary K. and welcomed her into this new phase of her life. I loved it when Nan, who is eighty-three, welcomed Mary K. into the company of "elders."

Some of the best rituals are not found in books. You can take special occasions into your own hands and make up rituals that fit the people and the occasion in a powerful and personal way.

Volume 7, Number 4, March–April 1985

Bishop of Justice

When through fiery trials thy pathways shall lie,
My grace, all sufficient, shall be thy supply;
The flame shall not hurt thee; I only design
Thy dross to consume, and thy gold to refine.

The moment was so filled with emotion that I burst into tears even now when I replay the videotape of it. At 8:38 p.m. on January 19, 1986, as the congregation packed into Duke University Chapel sang the verse of "How Firm a Foundation" quoted above, Bishop Desmond Tutu entered to the roar of the Chapel. The applause rose and mixed with singing as the bishop strode down the aisle, stopping only to greet a woman he seemed to know. While we finished the hymn he climbed to the pulpit to receive our applause.

Many of us had left home hours before and had waited first in the cold outside and then in the Chapel. The bishop's plane from Atlanta was late. By the time he arrived, we had run through all the scheduled hymns, anthems, prayers, announcements, and offering and were singing more hymns to fill up the time.

While we waited, I had time to recall stories I had heard about the efforts to integrate Duke Chapel in the early 1960s. I had time to think about the students on college campuses around the country who have taken up the banner of divestiture, this being the first clear public issue of right and wrong these children of Watergate have ever known.

The man who might otherwise be the leader of the antiapartheid movement, Nelson Mandela, has been in jail since before most of those students were born. So it falls to this clergyman, as it did to Martin Luther King Jr. in the United States, to be the public symbol of hope for a free South Africa.

Bishop Tutu thanked us for our support and spoke of a letter from a woman who prays for him daily in California. This support he compared to God's promise for the new Jerusalem found in Zechariah, "I will be like a wall of fire surrounding Jerusalem." Tutu said, "Those of us who are in situations of oppression know what it is to be upheld by the love and the prayers of their sisters and brothers scattered around the earth."

I guess we all expected Tutu to speak about the political situation in South Africa. He fooled us. Instead he talked about God, a God in whom I can believe and whose Christ I can claim. He spoke of the corporate nature of our life together, of a God who is always available and knows each of us by name, of a God who takes the side of the oppressed and calls each of us to be God's partner.

For Tutu, the most subversive thing about our faith is that it can say this to someone who has their dignity rubbed in the dirt and trampled underfoot: "Hey, you know something, mama?" (That's the old lady walking down the dusty streets of Soweto, whose name is not known by her employers because they say her real name is too difficult and so they call her Annie.) "Mama, as you walk down the street and they ask, 'Who is that?' You say, 'Oh, why that's God's partner.'"

Later, replaying a videotape of the evening, I realized that the woman the bishop stopped to greet was Motlalepula Chabaku who was recently granted political asylum from South Africa. When anyone asks her if there isn't something they can call her for short, Motlalepula replies, "They took my country away from me. They are not going to take my name. You can learn to say it, Mot-la-le-pu-la."

A woman prays for the bishop by name at 2:00 in the morning in the woods in California. The bishop chuckles and asks, "What chance does the South African government stand?"

Because he believes God takes the side of the oppressed, Tutu proclaimed near the end of his sermon, "We can say to the perpetrators of injustice and oppression anywhere and everywhere, 'You have already lost.'" And the bishop laughed out loud.

Volume 8, Number 3, January–February 1986

Turning Points

I was recently invited to preach at the ordination of a woman friend. As I prepared for that occasion, I kept wanting to call her up and say, "Tell me again why you want to be a minister."

The ordination of women is not brand new. Antoinette Brown Blackwell was ordained in a Congregational church in 1853. More recently, the Episcopal Church authorized the ordination of women in 1977. Even so, women in ministry have a hard time getting a job and an even harder time getting a second or third job that is different from the first. Women have to do any job twice as well as a man to be recognized as being half as good.

Women in ministry in the church today must be very brave. They are doing work that hardly anyone wants them to do.

Why would any bright, capable woman want to be a minister? Because she is a glutton for punishment? Because she heard voices? Because God called her? Why?

The church can feel like a very strange place for women. A favorite psalm of mine expresses the feeling I sometimes have.

> *By the waters of Babylon, there we sat down and wept, when we remembered Zion. On the willows there we hung up our lyres. For there our captors required of us songs, and our tormentors mirth, saying, "Sing us one of the songs of Zion." How shall we sing God's song in a foreign land?* (Psalm 137: 1–5)

The psalm describes a point in the story of the Hebrews when the people have a choice. They can choose to give up being who they are. They are already depressed, weeping for the loss of their land, their king, and their temple. They are in this terrible place called Babylon, and they can't figure out how to worship their God. They aren't even sure their God is still God in this strange place.

They can give up, or they can choose to change. They can sing the old songs louder than ever, sing old songs in new ways, or make up new songs altogether.

In the church today, we are at a turning point that is every bit as frightening, as challenging, and as exciting as the point at which the ancient Hebrew people hung up their lyres and wept.

What the psalm does not tell us is that in the years that followed, the Hebrews redefined themselves and their religion in response to the situation in which they found themselves. They developed synagogues as learning centers away from the temple in Jerusalem. They placed greater emphasis on the home as a center for religious education. They came to trust that their God was a God who could accompany them into foreign lands.

Had they not been able to change, we would probably never have heard of them or of Jesus.

Today we find ourselves in a world of change. Women, black people, third world people, poor people are all claiming a right to participate in the discussion about who God is.

Feminists are pushing for change in the church. We're not just talking about having more women in positions of leadership. It is not just about inclusive language. It's not just about referring to God as Mother and Father and to people as he and she. It's not just about whether Mary was a virgin or whether the disciples were male and female.

What we are after is a revolution. We mean to overthrow the hierarchy of God above minister, above men, above women, above children, above animals. We are talking about where God is located and about what the Trinity means and about whether monotheism is a good idea in the first place.

We are pushing out into the unknown with the blessing of a God who promised that revelation would continue and who promises to go with us into strange new places.

The church is not changing as fast as some of us would like. If we preach a sermon on any of the topics I just listed, we may have a riot on our hands. So why would any sane woman want to try? Why would she want to enter into the fray?

Precisely because it is one of the most exciting religious and cultural turning points in the history of the world. To be a spiritual leader with a vision of the future in this time is one of the most frightening and exciting challenges imaginable.

Change doesn't come easily. It wasn't easy for the Hebrews to find new ways to understand themselves. It is not easy for us, but it is the work God places before us to do.

We begin like the Hebrews by weeping. After we weep, after we weep each day for the injustice, inequity, and inhumanity we see around us, we call on the name of the God who created our lives and our world and who pronounced us good. We call up the vision of the God who brought us out of Egypt, out of bondage. We call on the sign of the God who promises to be faithful to us. We call on the God who hung on a cross and promised never to abandon us.

We sing God's song even in a strange land.

Volume 8, Number 5, May–June 1986

Klan

What do you do while the Ku Klux Klan rallies in your town?

As I leave my house with this question in mind this Sunday, June 7, 1987, it is the sound of the helicopters that makes the Klan's presence in our midst palpable to me. The last time the weekend quiet of downtown Greensboro, North Carolina, was interrupted by the whopwhop sound of choppers was November 4, 1979, the day after five members of the Communist Workers Party were shot and killed by Klansmen and Nazis.

Now, as then, a deadly quiet fills the streets around downtown. A police siren makes my heart stop, but it is headed away from town. Probably some tragedy we understand as routine—not this demonic power in our midst getting out of hand.

The police have blocked the streets into downtown for four blocks around the Klan rally at the governmental plaza in the center of town. I drive around the periphery of this ritual of death and wonder who the police are protecting. Are they protecting me from the Klan or the Klan from me? Or are they protecting the reputation of the city of Greensboro, badly damaged by the shootings here?

At any rate, I am glad that the police are there. I have visions of swarms of Klansmen being able to tell at a glance that I am a feminist and rolling my car. I can't, of course, see any Klansmen from this distance, but I can imagine.

I decide to join a small group in a prayer vigil in a church some distance from town. Another group of friends is present downtown, within sight of the beast, in silent vigil against the Klan. I am too disorganized (and too scared of ruining my summer vacation which starts in three days) to get that close to the beast. But I need to be with friends and to focus on this strange event in our midst.

The six of us sit quietly, praying, meditating, thinking, generating healing energy, whatever it is that people do as they sit quietly together. I am reminded of other times I have sat quietly with groups of people. I have sat most often with my friends, the Abu-Sabas. Mary is a native of Virginia. Elias, her husband, is from Lebanon. The death of a brother, a war, the murder of a mother—all these events brought a large, close-knit Lebanese family together to do what they seem to know how to do better than Americans: to sit quietly. I always want to *do* something.

Last week when this same Elias fell off a ladder and wound up in protracted back surgery, I found myself sitting quietly once again. What do you do for six hours while a friend, or husband, or brother is in surgery? What do you do for the afternoon while the Klan rallies in your town?

Very different situations, but ones in which I, we, my friends, have little control—for the moment.

I find that what I am able to do while the Klan is in our town is to feel how it feels. To feel how invaded it feels to have these strangers, most from outside Greensboro, in the middle of our home. It feels like a daytime version of finding a prowler in the living room in the wee hours of the morning. And yet, there is no breaking into Greensboro, only breaking into what I consider decency and justice and respect for the value of all human beings.

It feels like discovering that a peeping Tom has been watching at the bedroom window, that someone has found and read a private diary. It feels like being violated. How much more violated must the black families, or the Jewish families, or any of the other direct targets of the Klan feel?

At a North Carolina Women in Ministry Conference earlier this week, Linda Brown Bragg helped me to feel the violation blacks in this country have felt for generations. Reading aloud from her book *Rainbow Roun' Mah Shoulder* (Carolina Wren, 1984), Linda brought to life the grief, horror, and bewilderment of the family of a man who was killed by the Klan and the simple, graceful responses of neighbors and friends.

While still stunned by the horror of the scene Linda painted, my blurred senses met the sounds of a familiar hymn and the sight of a friend, Susan Thompson Moss, dancing silently to "Morning Has Broken." As this pale-skinned, blond-headed woman in yellow moved gracefully through her dance, I was both horrified by the contrast and warmed by the hope. In the face of the unspeakable, what we have is one another and one more day.

Volume 9, Number 5, May–June 1987

Holy Places

While in England and Norway this summer, I visited an assortment of holy places, including ancient stone circles, ruined abbeys, and one thousand-year-old churches.

My favorite, as I might have predicted, was the great stone circle, Stonehenge. Even in the rain, perhaps especially in the rain, this monument stands majestically on the Salisbury Plain. For thousands of years it has stood right there as a testimony to a people we know almost nothing about. I claim those people as my ancestors, for I am Scots-Irish and English. The people who built this and other stone circles in the British Isles were not the Celts but came before even those ancient ancestors.

The feeling was strong and clear for me that this was a holy place and had been a holy place for so long that it might as well have been forever. How many generations come and go in three thousand years? How many times would I have to say my grandmother's grandmother's grandmother to get back that far?

In addition to Stonehenge, I visited two other circles in England. (I was accused of wanting to see every rock in the countryside.) Avebury is a circle that encompasses several acres of ground. It is so large that a town called Avebury has grown up mingled with the stones. I also visited a much smaller circle that would fit easily in a modest backyard.

The ruined abbeys of England are another kind of holy place, from another period of history, but with a feeling similar to the stone circles. Tintern Abbey in Wales is one of many of the abbeys that Henry VIII stripped when he declared himself the head of the Church of English. Henry carried off everything that could be pried loose, including the roof and the windows. What remains is a kind of decaying lace work made of stone. As the viewer walks around the abbey, the arches play against one another in ever-changing patterns.

Compared to the dark, cold, damp cathedrals I visited, these skeletons seem light, airy and graceful. It is wonderful to see the sky through the top and the hills between the window arches. It occurred to me that churches might be much better without their windows or roofs.

The stone circles and the ruined abbeys had an open welcoming feeling about them that invited not only people but nature, the weather, and the seasons.

The third kind of holy place I visited and liked was a one thousand-year-old stave churches of Norway. Viking creations, they look like little trolls on the hillside with their dragon gargoyles and crosses. They are splendid examples of the blending of Christian and pagan symbols. The people of that land accepted Christianity but kept their former faith alive in this way.

In one small church a guide pointed out the large stone altar in the center and explained that the block of stone and its placement predated the church. A small well carved in the center of the stone allowed for the blood of sacrificed animals to drain away. I commented that it allowed the blood to reach mother earth. The guide looked at me as if I had lost my mind.

These early Norwegian churches are no longer in regular use. There is often a newer church close by, but they are still used for a service once a year on the celebration of the winter solstice.

I have a sense that the ancients knew something about spirituality that we have lost. Perhaps their experience of the divine was less abstract. As I stood in these holy places, I tried to imagine what people might have felt on a solstice long ago.

Volume 10, Number 1, September–October 1987

Clergywomen

Just after the first of the year a reporter came to see me to talk about a story on women in ministry. This reporter, like many before, asked what ought to be a simple question, How many women are there in ministry in the South? You would think the Resource Center for Women and Ministry in the South could answer a question like that, but we can't exactly.

One problem is that there is no one in the United States whose job it is to count these women. When the national media want to do a story on women in ministry, they do what the Resource Center does, which is call around to denominational agencies and try to get current figures.

The figures available are often like apples and oranges. One group may give you employed women ministers and another all living ministers. One may give you elders (fully ordained in some traditions) while others give you elders and deacons.

The Washington Post has estimated that there are about eight thousand women in ministry nationally. And how many might there be in the South? One could begin with the Southern Baptists, the largest Protestant denomination in the country. But the national convention is hostile towards women ministers, so they don't count them.

Here are figures the Resource Center has been able to collect on women in ministry. The columns in the chart represent the first year women were ordained or authorized, the number of ordained women, the total number of ordained ministers, the percentage women are of the total, and the year the figures represent.

	First Year Ordained	Number of Women Clergy	Total Number of Clergy	Percentage who are Women	Year of Report
American Baptist	*	199	6,600	3	1985
Disciples of Christ	1888	744	6,124	12	1987
Episcopal	1977	1,167	13,000	9	1987
Lutheran	1970	821	17,000	5	1987
PCUSA	1956	1,421	1 9,450	7	1987
Reform Jews	1972	101	1,450	7	1987
So. Baptist	1964	350	60,000	6	1987
UCC	1853	1,460	10,085	14	1986
United Methodist	1956	3,117	37,500	8	1986
Unitarian	1880	270	1,200	23	1987

Notes on chart:

American Baptists have allowed women's ordination for over 100 years.

The United Presbyterian Church, U.S.A. (ordained women in 1956) and the Presbyterian Church, U.S. (ordained women in 1964) now form the Presbyterian Church (U.S.A.)

Hostility toward women in ministry in the national Southern Baptist Convention and ordination by local congregations make accurate figures hard to get. The number is an estimate.

As the numbers of women in ordained ministry increase, the struggles of women continue. It will be some time before women have jobs, elected positions, and respect equal to our numbers and our capabilities. But some interesting things do happen to us along the way.

For the first time in the history of the National Council of Churches, a woman has been elected president. The Rev. Patricia McClurg, a Presbyterian, was elected in November 1987.

Helen Crotwell, a United Methodist district superintendent, is running for bishop in the Southeastern Jurisdiction. If elected, she would be the first woman bishop in the area. Only three clergywomen have ever been elected as bishops in the United Methodist Church, and as of August 1987 there were thirty-nine women district superintendents.

A joint mother-daughter ordination was celebrated in the Christian Church (Disciples of Christ) in June 1987 in Fullerton, California. Elaine Schoepf, 27, and her mother Gayle Schoepf, 57, became clergywomen together.

The following note appeared in a Pennsylvania church newsletter: "The January 3, 1988, installation of Reverend Carol Bernard as pastor of Trinity United Church of Christ has been temporarily postponed. Carol Bernard and her family are expecting the arrival of triplets in April 1988. Rev. Bernard will take a medical leave of absence beginning December 31, 1987. Plans for the installation will be announced at a later time."

Finally, The Central Committee of the World Council of Churches is sponsoring an Ecumenical Decade for Churches in Solidarity with Women that will begin at Easter 1988.

Volume 10, Number 3, January–February 1988

God(dess)

Note: A Presbyterian church I attended on a regular basis asked me to preach on language.

I am going to talk this morning about inclusive language and about images of God. This business of language is very important to me. If I left out why it was important to me and only gave you the ways I think we can fix it, you might be left with the answers to questions you never asked. So let me tell you why the content of religious language is important to me.

- Language like "The Fatherhood of God and the brotherhood of all mankind" makes it hard for me to worship, to feel connected.
- Accurate language is important in the education of children. Why make female children guess whether they are included or not?
- Generic words are not value free. Calling a photocopying machine a Xerox machine is not neutral. Referring to God as male confers added authority to men.
- Social reality informs our religious images and religious images reinforce our social reality.

The issue of religious language can be divided easily into two parts, language about humans and language about God. We in this church, as in many churches, are making good progress on language about people. I hear lots of ministers in all sorts of churches telling stories about men and women, about girls and boys, referring to the congregation as men and women and not just referring to the brotherhood of all mankind. So we are making progress.

Now for the second language issue, language about God. This one is currently the more difficult issue and the one that makes us all nervous. There are several possibilities for what we can do with language about

God. We have inherited several thousands of years of texts and traditions about God. Some people say that the weight of the tradition is such that we should use "father" and other male language about God. But tradition is not reason enough. Tradition used to demand that we use "Thee" and "Thou" for God and not drive cars on Sunday. The tradition changes.

One thing we can do is use gender inclusive language for God. Those of you who were here last Sunday morning heard Tim Kimrey, one of the ministers of this church, say something about "God . . . She . . ." and not miss a beat. Did anybody notice that but me?

We can sort of mix up our use of gender language. We can sometimes use She for God and sometimes He. We can refer to God as Mother, Father, and Our Maker. We have already begun to pray, "Our Maker who art in heaven." Did you notice that one? There are ways we can describe God that give us back some of the feminine images that have been lost in our tradition.

Another thing we can do besides being more gender inclusive in our language is to actively seek images in scripture where God is portrayed in a feminine or female or mothering role. I never can find these when I want them, so I thought I would just list a few of them for you.

- In Isaiah 42:14 God is described as a pregnant woman,
- In Isaiah 66:13 as a mother, and
- In Psalm 22:9 as a midwife.
- In Luke 13:31–35 God is described as a brood hen trying to gather her chicks under her wing.

These are metaphors we find in scripture that we can use. If we used them on a regular basis our image of God might be enlarged. We would show that God can be both father and mother, both male and female.

But I have finally decided that the big problem is the name we use for God. Just about a week ago, I realized that G-o-d is the proper name for a male deity in our tradition. G-o-d is the name we give to our deity. Our Jewish brothers and sisters don't even try to say the name God because the name of God is so holy. They say "Adonai," which is translated in English as "the Lord." Christians took great liberty with God's name and called God Jehovah and later Yahweh, both of which are poor attempts to try to pronounce an unpronounceable name which had four consonants and no vowels. We have taken to calling God, God. That is the name for our deity.

Webster's will tell you there is a word for a deity that is feminine. (Hold onto your hats.) The word is *Goddess*. Try changing the language in the hymns from God to Goddess and from Lord to Lady and see what the people around you do. They may think you have wandered into the wrong century or the wrong place.

So to use a word like Goddess, which ought to be a female equivalent for God, makes us nervous. If using Goddess wasn't really loaded, then it wouldn't make us shiver and make me nervous even to suggest it. I can hardly imagine what it would be like to come to church on Sunday morning and have all the God language be Goddess language and have Lord be replaced by Lady. We should try it sometime just as an experiment.

The interesting question is why this makes us so nervous. This is not a new nervousness. It is thousands of years old. It is something that came about in a very intentional and logical way. How is it that we wound up with a language and a set of images that are so overwhelmingly male? And why are we so nervous about this word Goddess?

Well, there was a time in the Holy Land when God was a woman, or when the supreme deity that was worshipped was female. Her name was Asherah. You can find her in the Hebrew scriptures. Funny how she is never portrayed in a very good light in Scripture. She is often the one the Hebrew prophets are telling about. You have probably heard of her male colleague, Baal.

Asherah is mentioned by name or by reference about forty times in the Hebrew Scriptures. She is always a temptation to the Israelites. And few of the references to her appear in our lectionary. That means you could go to church every Sunday of the world and never hear there was a

Goddess—good, bad, or indifferent. So, I feel a little like I am telling you a secret somebody didn't want you to know.

I want you to hear a few of the references to her. In Jeremiah 44:15–19 the Hebrew people are scolded for making cakes for the Queen of Heaven. The people have been drug off down to Egypt and they are really mad at Jeremiah for not getting them out. So they take up with their old religion. Jeremiah protests and the people say, "But we will do everything that we have vowed, burn incense to the Queen of Heaven and pour out libations to her, as we did . . . in the cities of Judah and in the streets of Jerusalem; for then we had plenty of food and prospered, and saw no evil."

In I Kings 14:23, the people are putting up "asherim." To make a Hebrew noun plural, you add "im." People were going around putting up posts or wooden symbols of Asherah "on every high hill and under every green tree."

In Hosea 2, Hosea is calling his wife, Gomer, a harlot, because she is a priestess of the Goddess and goes back home to her people periodically to perform her rites. Her rites sometimes get her pregnant. Hosea calls her a whore. She wasn't a whore, she was a priestess in the Canaanite fertility religion. There is a difference. So the next time you read about Gomer, think of her as the minister at the church down the road.

Now, the Hebrews had a brilliant scheme to make their faith unique and make it resistant to being assimilated into any other religion. It is part of what has carried the tradition forward for thousands of years. The plan had two parts.

The first part was monotheism. "There is only one God. We've got the God. If you have a god by another name or a goddess, you have nothing, no god at all." I'm not sure this was such a good idea, because it has allowed people ever since to say, "We've got the God, you've got nothing, so you are nothing, so we can do to you whatever we want." There may come a time when we either see all the gods as part of the same god or we may have to agree to recognize other people's gods.

The second thing they did was to make their God overwhelmingly male so that their God could not be confused with Asherah, the fertility goddess of the Canaanites. The religion of the Hebrews developed in the face of the Canaanite fertility religion that honored the cycle of the seasons and worshipped female deities along with male ones. Describing God as male ensured that the God of the Hebrews could not be confused in any way with the Goddess of the Canaanites.

What we are left with several thousand years later in Christianity and in Judaism are symbols, metaphors, language, and stories that are thoroughly masculine. (The female images I offered earlier do not begin to outweigh this.) This overwhelmingly male language makes it hard for women to make a connection to our own female selves.

That is why I care about this matter. If you think that I am all hung up on this, you are right. I am so hung up that when I try to worship in a church that talks about the "Fatherhood of God" and the "brotherhood of all mankind," it really gets in my way. I feel so alienated and shut out that I can't worship at all.

Now we may have a problem if you are a person who can't worship in a church that prays to God as Mother and Father, or God as Maker, or God as Creator. If you don't like to hear about the brotherhood and sisterhood of all humankind, then we may be in trouble. How are you and I going to get along in the same place? And what if we are both good Presbyterians and feel like we each have a right to be in this church? What are we going to do?

I come to *this* church because I believe that it is a community in process. I'll keep lobbying to change "all mankind" to "humankind" in the closing hymn. I'll try to keep a sense of humor and continue to believe that neither God nor the Goddess is finished with any of us.

We are on a journey. We are not alone. She is with us. Amen.

Volume 12, Number 1, September–October 1989

Empty Seats

Note: I lived in Philadelphia for most of 1990. I thought South of the Garden *readers might enjoy reading what I thought of Easter in the North.*

Remember the children's hand game, "Here's the church, and here's the steeple. Open the door and here are all the people." If you clasp your hands with the fingers in, when you open them up you see all the little finger-people. But if you clasp your hands normally, when you open them up it is empty inside.

Well, that's sort of what it is like with churches up here in the North. I once heard a Northerner standing in Duke Chapel ask, "So, what do you do with this place on Sundays?" The visitor was shocked at the answer, "Fill the place up." I've always heard that people in the North don't go to church like people in the South, but I didn't have a picture of what that meant.

Easter tells a lot. I've been attending this great church, First United Methodist Church of Germantown (FUMCOG), where I went on Ash Wednesday. Fifteen or twenty folks attended. I thought, "That's fine, Methodists are not big on Ash Wednesday." I later attended a Maundy Thursday service and again, about twenty or twenty-five people were there.

On Good Friday I went right around the corner from where I live to Christ Episcopal Church, the oldest Episcopal church in Phila-delphia. What a gorgeous old church it is with large windows and those marble things that look like tomb stones all over the walls like in the cathedrals in England. Anyway, the church was having a Tenebrae service, a service of readings, music, silence, and darkness. It was beautiful. The Philadelphia Brass Ensemble played "Oh Sacred Head Now Wounded." The choral music was gorgeous: Bach, Handel, etc. The service started at 7:30 p.m., so it got dark outside as the service went on. It was wonderful. Again, only a smattering of people attended.

I had this great idea to go to Bethlehem, Pennsylvania, to the Moravian sunrise service on Easter morning. The Easter sunrise service with the Moravians in Winston-Salem, North Carolina, is quite an event. In Winston-Salem, brass bands walk through neighborhoods well before dawn calling people out. Everyone gathers on the green in front of Home Moravian Church. After some readings, what seems like hundreds of brass instruments lead the worshippers to God's Acre (the cemetery) for more music, readings, and prayers.

I went to Bethlehem, spent the night, got up at 4:30 a.m., and arrived at Central Moravian Church at 5:00 a.m. to get a seat for the 5:30 service. A seat? There were enough seats left over for everyone to have five or six. And there were only about eight brass instruments. It was raining so we did not go out to God's Acre. They did serve Moravian sugar cake afterwards, but it was a little dried out and had cinnamon on it. We don't put cinnamon on it in North Carolina.

After the sugar cake, I went back to bed for a little while and overslept, so I had to rush back to Philadelphia (over an hour away). When I realized I was going to be late, I worried that I would never get a seat. Then I remembered that I was in the North. Sure enough, fifteen minutes late on Easter Sunday morning I had no trouble getting a seat in what I think is one of the most exciting churches in town. If I'd been fifteen minutes late to any of the churches I have ever attended in the South, I'd have been propped up on the radiator.

Easter evening arrived, and I still wanted more. I walked a few blocks to a jazz vespers service at Old Pine Presbyterian Church, a beautifully restored historic church. The sanctuary is so lovely to look at that I would pay money just to sit in it. For over an hour I listened to the most wonderful jazz, prayers, and meditations. The congregation? Well, it was embarrassing. I think it was actually a pretty good showing. It looked like the number of folks you might expect for the early morning service in late August (the week everyone goes on vacation) in a church in the South.

I don't mean to sound cruel. It's just that I can't get over the fact that there are all these splendid religious offerings, the likes of which it is hard to come by in the South, and so few people who attend.

I don't know exactly what to make of the regional differences. It does make me think that working in the church in the South is important because people still participate there.

Even so, churches in the South complain about not having enough members. They should see what it is like in a big northern city. They could even take a lesson from their northern cousins and try some serious recruitment programs. A church like FUMCOG does not let a single visitor go unnoticed. If they did, in spite of great preaching, music, and community, they might go out of business.

When the mail arrived on Easter Monday, it contained something that really cheered me up: a big white candy Easter cross. It was so silly and so southern it almost made me cry.

Volume 12, Number 4, May–June 1990

The Art of Feeding the Spirit

At conferences, I am always drawn to workshops where we get to draw, make things, sing, or dance. I learn things about myself in those settings, and it's better than endless hours of verbal input.

In May, the Resource Center sponsored a conference called "The Art of Feeding the Spirit." We designed the conference to explore the connection between the arts and spirituality. Since the conference, I have been thinking about what I learned.

I enjoyed the conference. I especially liked a workshop led by Adele Wayman, a Greensboro artist. She showed slides of goddess images and of art by women. Then she laid out paper, fabric, string, and glue and told us to make something. I made a torn paper picture that reflects where I am in my own life. Since the conference, I have found myself decorating postcards and letters in an attempt to express my creativity.

In addition to a renewed appreciation for creative expression as a part of a spiritual life, I discovered something else. I learned to look more carefully at what feeds my spirit on a daily basis.

One thing that feeds my spirit is a connection to the earth. When I was in college, I took a class on Zen Buddhism from a Japanese American professor of religion. He used to say that his church was the woods. I thought that was wonderful for people who weren't Christian or Jewish.

I have argued against the notion that church only exists inside the walls of a building marked "church." Still, I have clung to notions of religiosity. I have been a little afraid to say what feeds me spiritually.

I accuse patriarchal religion of stuffing spirituality into predefined boxes and telling us to do it a certain way. Though I thought I had expanded my understanding of spirituality, I think I've been stuck with a notion that spiritual activities have to be identifiably religious.

Sitting on the front porch at lunchtime, looking out the window at a dogwood tree, watching the seasons change on the landscape of a park, digging in the dirt—all these things nurture me. I have known they were important, but I did not realize how much I depend on them for my connection to the spirit and to myself.

Realizing the importance of my connection to the earth has helped me to understand why it is so hard for me to live in the downtown of a big city. Trees and grass have always been part of my life and of my sense of well-being. Now I make daily pilgrimages to a path along the Schuylkill River where grass and trees grow. We are making common cause. I don't think the trees like the city very much either.

I was especially helped to see the connection between the earth and my spirituality by one of the conference leaders, Lynne Crow. Having sat at the feet of many a Native American wise woman, Lynne shared some of her insights with us. I already understood that Native American tradition honored nature, but Lynne taught me to talk to the trees, to the rivers, and to the animals. She says they like to hear our voices and that the native peoples of this continent used to talk to them regularly. The trees wonder if we are human, since we usually just look at them.

The earth feeds me. Different things feed different people. I know a woman who likes to sing. If she does not get to sing with the choir on Wednesday night and Sunday morning, she is very unhappy. Some people are fed by dancing, or meditating, or writing; some by the ocean; others by a landscape. I've even found other folks who share my attachment to the Texas prairie.

I seem to be discovering a spirituality that is rooted in daily life. Sunlight in the morning, good food, visits with friends, and long walks—all of these feel like parts of a spiritual discipline. I'm not interested in a privatistic piety, but I would like for walking in the woods, painting a picture, and writing a poem to rank up there with talking to God on our knees.

Volume 12, Number 5, July–August 1990

Forty

I've come to recognize the feeling. I get up in the morning. I look in the closet, and I hate all my clothes. Then I remember: I'm going to start my period. I didn't hate my clothes yesterday, but today I would like to put them all in a cardboard box and take them to Goodwill. I have to wear clothes, so I put something on. I look dowdy. Oh, well. I don't mind menstruating, you understand. I just hate having nothing to wear.

There is a new feeling these days that I don't recognize. I hate my job. It's the same job it was last year. It's the same job it was ten years ago. It's just as hard to raise money now as it was then. It's just as much fun to be my own boss now as it was then. Then I remember: I turned forty this year.

I hate it when I realize that I am part of a demographic trend. Like everyone else in my graduating class, I wanted to be *different*. But just like lots of other people my age, it is a little harder to see to read than it used to be, and there is a gnawing sense of meaninglessness around the edges of my life.

I once felt the years and options spread out endlessly before me like a west Texas landscape. Now I feel like the end of the road is nearly in sight.

Never having had children, this last birthday seems particularly poignant. People are constantly telling me about a friend who had her first baby at forty-six. "The exception that proves the rule," I think to myself. I might, in fact, still conceive and bear a child, but I cannot get over the feeling that the eggs I produce now are numbered and that the countdown is approaching single digits.

OK, so being forty means that I no longer have infinite options.

I got a newsletter from my college recently. Inside were big pictures of intelligent-looking young people. I expected to read that these were scholarship recipients or winners of some award. I was shocked to read that they were the newest members of the faculty. Holy smoke! They look like kids. As I read over their credentials, I learned that they earned college degrees in 1983, 1984, 1986. Oh, there's one who graduated in 1973 like me. She looks thoughtful, not too old.

I had a conversation with two young people the other day. One was twenty-five years old, the other thirty. Their energy almost made me tired. I am now less willing to throw myself into things than I once was. Less willing to go to meetings at night. Less willing to sign up to volunteer for this or that. Less willing to do it over again like last year. Now more than ever, I am impatient to know what is worth doing.

I'm not exactly the same person I have been, but I'm not sure who I am becoming either. Carolyn Heilbrun, the writer, assures women that being fifty-plus is marvelous. So I have great things to look forward to, if I survive being forty.

Volume 13, Number 5, December 1991

Hamlet

In April I heard two survivors of the poultry plant fire in Hamlet, North Carolina, speak. Each told of the horror of being trapped behind locked doors. Of the cries. Of thinking that the end was surely here. These were two of the lucky ones. Another twenty-five were not so lucky. All because the doors were locked—so people would not steal chickens, the managers said. One of the women said that she had worked a lot of places and had never been treated so badly. Women were not allowed to go to the bathroom without permission and sometimes had to pee on the floor. It was a terrible place before the fire. Now it is a terrible symbol of inhumane treatment of working people in our land.

I went to Hamlet in early May. I have been interested in poultry workers for ten years, ever since I first heard a group of poultry workers from eastern North Carolina describe the terrible conditions in the plants. All day with your hands in freezing cold water. Over a hundred chickens whizzing by every minute to inspect. Salmonella everywhere. Conditions are just as bad for the chickens and for the boys who catch the chickens in the chicken houses. The growers who incubate the chicks get a pretty raw deal as well. It is a miserable industry.

After I heard the two survivors of the Hamlet fire speak, I decided to go with friends to a march and rally in Hamlet on May 2. We talked politics for the two hours it took to drive to Hamlet, which is due south, just off US 1, almost to the South Carolina state line. It was a beautiful day. It was not hard to find the town or the plant. Many of the fifteen hundred people at the march were union folks. They came from Michigan and Illinois, New York and Florida. It was a great gathering of people who are deeply involved in the labor movement.

As folks were gathering in the dusty parking lot in front of the old brick plant, one member of our group got nosy and decided she would poke around the building. Sure enough, she and some other folks found a way in. I went, too.

I reached the back of the building, as big as an airplane hanger, and made my way in through an open door. It was pitch dark inside. My friend said to wait until my eyes adjusted. I had to stand there for a minute. I could not see at all. I could feel a step with my toe and stepped up before I could see anything. As my eyes began to adjust, I found myself in a concrete room that looked like a boiler room, with pipes and big metal machines. There was a lot of water on the floor in the middle of the room and there were some other people coming towards me through the water. They said it was not deep, just slippery. My friend said we should go through the water and around the corner to see the frying room, where she thought the fire actually started.

I walked the length of a room that looked like a boiler room to me. I rounded the corner. What lay before me is hard to describe. A huge black machine, black from the smoke of the fire. There was a large container, with pipes and valves around it, all out of joint and twisted. That must have been the fryer. Above it was an enormous hole in the roof with sunlight pouring in. A cavernous room, black as coal, lit from above by the light of day. Behind me in the other direction was total darkness.

It was like being in the belly of the beast.

We looked for a while and left by the same way we had entered, through the room with water on the floor. As I neared the exit I noticed my feet were wet and greasy. I can't get rid of the sensation of greasy shoes. It was as though the screams and the terror and the chickens and the cruelty clung to my shoes. I wanted to wash the dirty water out of my shoes, and the death and destruction off my hands.

Outside it was bright and dry and everything seemed orderly enough. I turned to my friends and said, "Yea, though I walk through the valley of the shadow of death. . . ." They laughed nervously.

Note: Adapted from a sermon preached May 3, 1992, at the Church of Reconciliation in Chapel Hill, North Carolina.

Volume 14, Number 2, June 1992

Voice

I was invited to preach in a large Baptist church in Charlotte, North Carolina, in September of this year. As I got ready to write a sermon for the occasion, I found myself writing the kind of background comments that precede the actual writing of a presentation. This windup interested me more than usual, so I decided to share some of it with you. It is, as you will see, about a woman trying to find her voice. I was imagining myself standing in the pulpit.

No one ever meant for me to stand in this place.
- Certainly not the designer of this pulpit, or it would have been built so that I could see the first three rows of the congregation.
- Not the people who built this church. Fifty years ago, though there were Baptist and Presbyterian women missionaries, there were almost no ordained women in the mainline Protestant denominations in this country.
- I would be surprised if any of the folks who met on the campus of a women's college to begin this congregation imagined that a short Presbyterian woman minister would ever stand in this place.

No one in my family ever imagined I would stand in this place, not even the women.
- Not my great-grandmother who was born near Charlotte and whose family followed the Scots-Irish migration west to Arkansas and then Texas.
- Not my grandmother who led the choir in her Presbyterian church in Itasca, Texas, for thirty-five years. She taught me the *Children's Catechism* and gave me a love for the church. She adored me but never imagined me as a preacher.
- Not even my mother who took me to church every Sunday of the world. She told me I should do whatever I wanted with my life but never imagined this is what I'd choose.

It is an accident of history that I came along at exactly the time when women began to enter graduate and professional schools in larger numbers than ever before. I picked seminary. I almost went to law school or graduate school in mathematics instead.

Neither the fine people who began this church nor the fine women of my family ever meant for us to be together like this today. But here we are, by the grace or the clever plotting of God. Now we are to make church together, to worship God. This may not be an easy task.

What if my height or voice or gender make it hard for you to worship? What if my presence in this place, where I was never meant to stand, is as problematic for you as the beautiful but overwhelming architecture of this church is for me?

What if you have as much trouble finding your own sense of worship in my presence as I do in finding my voice in this building? You see, I currently go to church in a low gray wooden building. The sanctuary doubles as a fellowship hall and has a concrete floor and movable chairs. People dress informally, come late and leave early, and children have been seen wandering around during the service. (Don't get me wrong, I'm not blaming the Baptists for screwing the pews to the floor. I understand that Presbyterians can take full credit for that.)

What if the color of my robe, royal purple, disturbs you?

Our assignment to be the church together, in the latter years of the twentieth century, is one of the hardest we have had since the Protestant churches split over slavery. We don't agree anymore. In the same congregation, we don't agree, not about worship, not about politics. Some of us think worship should be quiet and meditative. Some think festive and energizing. Some want words, some want almost no words. Some want inclusive language, some don't.

Into this moment shaped by history and tradition, I am to speak. It is no surprise that it is sometimes hard for a woman to find her voice.

Volume 14, Number 4, November 1992

Choice

In the fall of 1972, my father, then an obstetrician and gynecologist in Tulsa, Oklahoma, was indicted for performing illegal abortions. It was in the papers. I remember feeling embarrassed, even though I was away at college. He and my mother had been divorced for several years, and I was not in very close touch with him.

I also felt just a little proud of him. I was glad that there was someone competent performing abortions, if he was. I never really learned the truth. He was never brought to trial. There was a case pending in the Supreme Court at the time. It was, of course, Roe v. Wade. On January 22, 1973, the Supreme Court decided to legalize abortion and my father returned from semi-outlaw status to just plain doctor again.

I was one of the lucky ones. I never had an unwanted pregnancy. In 1973 I thought the matter had been settled once and for all. Abortions were going to be safe, legal, and available (at least in the earlier stages of pregnancy) in the land. Little did I know that for sixteen of the next twenty years Republican administrations would do everything in their power to erode the availability of abortions. Little did I know that what felt like a personal issue for me as a woman and as a doctor's daughter would become one of the hottest political issues of our time.

For the last twenty years groups such as NARAL (National Abortion Rights Action League), RCAR (Religious Coalition for Abortion Rights), and Planned Parenthood have fought to keep abortion safe and legal. For twenty years they have withstood threats, letter bombs, Operation Rescue, grisly pictures of fetuses, and being called murderers. Doctors who were willing to perform abortions in clinics have been personally harassed. One doctor's children were scared out of their wits by protestors in their own front yard. Access to abortion has been seriously eroded.

With the stroke of a pen, on January 22, 1993, twenty years to the day from the original Roe v. Wade decision, Bill Clinton has stemmed the tide. No longer will the administration be working to make abortions inaccessible. Anti-choice people know it, too. Anti-choice protestors marching in Washington on January 22, 1993, were quoted as saying that they knew they would get little legislative help in the near future.

The coalition between big business and the religious right that swept Ronald Reagan into power and put a twelve-year stranglehold on freedom, justice, and equality is now in disrepair and defeat. The religious right has come under general public suspicion. Many of its leaders are in disgrace.

I now breathe air that feels fresher and freer. Finally, perhaps for the first time since Roe v. Wade was decided, we can get on to the work that all of us have wanted to do all along: addressing the causes of unwanted pregnancies. Lack of education, too little birth control, poverty, low self-esteem, and incest are among the causes of teenage pregnancy. Even correcting these problems won't eliminate all unwanted pregnancies, or all the need for abortion, but it will go a long way in that direction.

It is our job to restore to women more than just their right to choose, more than their bodies. We must also help restore to women their souls, their ability to take up for themselves, to take care of their bodies, and to honor themselves. We need to protect the integrity of women. Body and soul.

Volume 15, Number 1, February 1993

Epiphany

Christmas vacation 1992 was a pilgrimage to my roots. I visited family in Texas and Oklahoma and went to the churches of my childhood. One of these churches was my grandmother's church, a small-town southern Presbyterian church in Texas, with a stained-glass Jesus praying on a rock. The other, Southminster Presbyterian, was a modern suburban church in Tulsa, Oklahoma, where I grew up.

Sitting in the sanctuary of Southminster on Christmas Eve, I found myself wondering what it was I wanted from the church. I felt like there was something I wanted the church to give me or to tell me, but I wasn't sure exactly what.

It was not until Epiphany, twelve days later, that the light broke through my fog and I realized what I had been looking for. It seems so obvious now. I was looking for the church's blessing. I realized that the church had always held out some sort of promise to me, a promise to be a home, to be a place of acceptance, like it had been in my childhood.

I went back to the churches of my childhood wondering if I had been mistaken. Had I read the signals wrong? Had I been deluding myself? No, the church had been a safe place for me as a child. In the one in Tulsa, I had even been encouraged to think for myself, to ask questions, to use my imagination.

Sitting in the church in Tulsa on Christmas Eve, I felt like Jacob at the Jabbok River, wrestling with the angel. It was as though I had the church by the shoulders and was shaking it, saying, "Give it to me."

I am not sure what the church could give me now that would make up for what it did not give me when I was preparing to be ordained. The minister of my home church offered no support while I was in seminary, even though I was the only seminarian from that church at the time. Presbytery officials told me the churches did not really want women ministers. The ministers of the church in Greensboro, North Carolina, where I belonged while I was a candidate for ordination paid very little attention to me. When I was finally ordained in 1982, a friend in the congregation had to call the ministers and remind them that they were required to recognize me in some formal way. They invited me to read scripture one morning at the eleven o'clock service.

The tenth anniversary of my ordination was last fall. I found myself unwilling to attend the Presbytery meeting where my name was read aloud with others celebrating anniversaries. My response to the whole thing was to cry. I felt like they had no right to call my name and say congratulations when for the five years I spent trying to get ordained and for the ten years since the institutional church has been less than helpful.

Friends ask why we stay with it. Why do we keep hammering away at the church until it blesses us or we change it? I don't know the answer.

I still long for something, some blessing. All Jacob got from the angel was a wound and his name. I guess that is what I have also. I have certainly been wounded in the struggle with the church. I suppose I also have the church to thank for my name. The church still defines me. It still calls me by name. I still belong, even as One Who Makes Change. Maybe the church did make good on its promise after all, just not the way I had in mind.

Volume 15, Number 1, February 1993

Creativity

I have been writing every morning for the last six months. Three pages longhand. What do I write? Whatever comes into my head. When nothing comes into my head, I write the names of vegetables in alphabetical order.

I have added writing to my morning routine which already included a half-hour walk. Some mornings the routine of getting ready for the day seems like it takes longer than the day itself.

In the fall I began reading *The Artist's Way: A Spiritual Path to Higher Creativity*, by Julia Cameron (Tarcher/Perigee, 1992). The book recommends this practice of writing three pages every morning. Having written a journal off and on for several years, I decided to try it. I loved it immediately and am now addicted. The practice of writing has kept my internal conversation going in a more organized way. Cameron recommends using the time to complain and to write whatever you feel, so that the creative work of the day can proceed with fewer blocks. She also includes exercises in the twelve-week program that help you deal with negative voices within, with a variety of blocks to creativity, and with the fear of success.

I find reading about writing almost as addictive as the writing practice itself. I checked a bunch of books on writing out of the library and then bought copies of the ones I liked the best. I have become a fan of two women who write about writing, Natalie Goldberg and Brenda Ueland. Goldberg's *Writing Down the Bones* (Shambhala, 1986) and Ueland's *If You Want to Write* (Graywolf, 1987) are wonderful books about the process of writing. Neither of these is about the structure of language. Both are about the spirituality of writing.

Goldberg has published a new book that is as much about her life as about writing, *Long Quiet Highway* (Bantam, 1994). I enjoyed it very much, particularly the connection between Zen practice and writing practice. Don't let the story in the beginning about the monks who jog over a mountain every night scare you off.

Ueland writes about the daily necessity for "moodling." You know what moodling is. It is doodling without a pencil. It is muddling around. It is easier for me to do on vacation, but I need to do it every day. I need lots of unfocused, unprogrammed time; otherwise there is no place for new ideas to take root.

I've also gotten interested in this cultural plague of busy-ness. Trying to find time in each day to write, walk, and moodle makes it painfully obvious how busy I like to stay. I've started reading Anne Wilson Schaef's *Meditations for Women Who Do Too Much* (Harper & Row, 1990). People who know me would never accuse me of being a workaholic, but I do tend to keep moving and to keep busy. Slowing down, writing, walking, and moodling have become the new ingredients of my spiritual practice.

The Resource Center is sponsoring a retreat at the beach May 30–June 1, 1993. The theme is "Body & Soul." We recommend that people read *The Artist's Way* ahead of time. We plan to be quiet together. To walk on the beach. To talk about our bodies, our faith, and our spiritual practice. The planning committee keeps saying that the ocean will be the main speaker. We will also have resource people. Mel Bringle, author of *The God of Thinness* (Abingdon, 1992), will speak about bodies. Others will lead movement, meditation, massage, and ritual. But if you want to come and just listen to the ocean, that is OK, too.

Volume 15, Number 2, April 1993

Gloria

As I sit in a brand new auditorium on the campus on North Carolina State University in an audience of mostly nice-looking ladies, I wonder what Gloria Steinem might say. Will this almost fifty-nine-year-old Smith College graduate, who wears her hair falling down in her face and founded *Ms. Magazine*, have anything to say that will make it worth a whole Tuesday morning? By the time the lecture begins, there are people sitting in the aisles and standing in the back of the five hundred-seat auditorium. A lot of other folks think Gloria might be worth a Tuesday morning. The woman sitting next to me is saying to a friend, "I just don't see how someone like Gloria Steinem could have ever had low self-esteem."

The introductions begin. This is a promotional tour for her book, *Revolution from Within* (Little, Brown and Co., 1992). The book store owner doing the introduction says that a generous donation will be made to the local battered women's shelter as a result of this event. I like that.

Gloria takes the microphone. She has her hair pulled back. I can see her face. I'm glad. (I sound like my mother.) It is a warm face. Gloria apologizes for being in an auditorium with the chairs screwed to the floor. She would like for us to be facing one another. She says that we are the point here, not she. Her role as an outside agitator is to get all of us together to realize that we don't need an outsider. She suggests that we might want to turn this into an organizing meeting to get rid of Jesse Helms. The audience applauds wildly. She promises to leave time at the end for local announcements, political pleas, and sharing ideas.

Oh, good. She understands about groups. She cares about what happens to these people who are in her care for the next hour or so.

Before she gets very far into her comments, a baby near the front of the audience begins to cry. The mother rises to take the child from the room. Gloria stops, turns to the woman, and says, "Please don't leave. We put up with unpleasant noises all the time. This is a pleasant one. It will be all right. Really." All of a sudden I feel like I want to cry. This level of kindness takes me by surprise.

She has been touring the country for a year now, talking about her book. What she has learned from the women she has talked with in towns and cities across the land is that they appreciate knowing that she has felt insecure in her life. They feel braver by knowing that they are not the only scared ones. They, like the woman sitting next to me, must have thought that all feminists were born brave.

Gloria says that the personal is political. We know that. In her year of touring she has discovered that we have done better on the political part than the personal part. We now have large national political organizations such as NOW, the Women's Political Caucus, and Emily's Fund. But we have lost track of the personal. We need to go back to where the women's movement began. We need more opportunities for small groups where we can say, "You feel like that? I thought I was the only one who felt like that."

She thinks the golden rule was developed for men. For women, it should be to treat ourselves as well as we treat others. Gloria's advice is to build a small group into your life.

She covers other issues like violence and child-raising practices. Before she ends her remarks, she encourages us to each do one outrageous thing this week. Then she shares with us her rules for living and changing the world:

- give ten percent of your salary to social justice,
- write five letters or post cards a week to elected officials to thank them or to express your views,
- vote, and
- attend one demonstration a month to keep your blood tingling.

Volume 15, Number 2, April 1993

Summer

For two weeks this summer, I sat in a white Adirondack chair on a screened porch and stared at a bush. It was not just any bush. A white oleander bush in the front yard of a rented cottage on Ocracoke Island off the coast of North Carolina.

I sat. With my notebook lying open on the wide flat arm of the chair, I sat. Because the bush was magical. Because gravity exaggerated the slope of the chair and made it hard to get up. Because I wanted to hear the inside of my head. I sat.

Oh, I walked on the beach every day, played in the surf, and watched the sun set slowly over a picture-perfect harbor. But mostly I sat and stared at that bush.

I wrote some. It mattered little what I wrote. What mattered was sitting and not wanting to be anywhere else.

I remember a feeling I often had in college, that the action was happening somewhere else. I would ride the bus from my women's college to the men's college nearby, certain that if something was going to happen, it would happen to me there. I was still under the illusion that "it" was "out there" somewhere. It's not. I learn that simple fact over and over in a thousand different ways. "It" is inside.

I find that inner peace all too infrequently. I long for the feeling of being in the right place. I knew the feeling as a small child, wrapped up in a bath towel and my mother's gentle arms, sculpting art out of dough scraps in my grandmother's kitchen, telling stories to the dolls in my room. I remember what it felt like to be at home.

I have that feeling too rarely now. The sense of not wanting or needing to be anywhere else. When the oughts and the lists and the need to improve all fall away.

I guess that is why I need a summer vacation. To stop, if only for a moment, the impulse to make widgets. To stare at a rock, a river, or a tree. To know God in the being rather than in the striving.

That's what I found in a chair, on a porch, by a bush, on an island in the middle of the sea.

Volume 15, Number 3, August 1993

AΩ (Alpha Omega)

Dying is like being born. A woman might not agree to give birth but the baby finally makes her so uncomfortable that she says, "Let's get on with it." We would never let people go, but they help us. We cannot bear to watch them suffer. Or they get weaker and weaker and fade away slowly and we get ready.

Dying and being born. How alike they are. And now for you it is all happening at once. Your father is leaving this world and your child is arriving. As the child grows larger and stronger, drawing on your own body for its life, your father grows weaker. He gave you life and now you give it to another. As his light grows dimmer, this child's grows brighter. As the life force slips out of him, it slips into this child. Dying and being born. The pain, the joy, the sadness, the overwhelming nature of it all.

Along with them you are also dying and being born. Don't be so good. Don't take such good care of all of us. Fall apart. A little girl is losing her daddy and her heart is breaking just as surely as if your own child were losing you. It is almost too much to take in all at once. But let it in. In these days as we approach the solstice, you stand in the midst of life's most powerful events. If you feel you cannot stand up sometimes, it is because the strongest tides the human spirit ever feels are tugging at your ankles.

There is nothing to do but feel it. Feel it every day. The joy and the sorrow. The baby's kicking, a child's laughter, the sadness, and the loss. It is all right there, splashed in bright colors on the canvas of your heart. Your heart can hold it, though it feels that it is breaking. You have the biggest heart I know. In fact, your heart can only hold it all by breaking apart and growing larger. So in these days of your breaking heart remember that you are well loved by God, by your dad, by your family, and by your friends. Let this love lift you up on wings like the wings of the morning and bear you gently as you weep and wait.

This is a time for roaring, for weeping, for wailing, for being quiet, and for waiting. The roaring of the wind in your ears is the sound of the spirits rushing into and out of this world. If your father and the baby never meet each other, know that their spirits passed each other and spoke on the highway that leads into and out of this life. They will always know each other. Their spirits live very close together now. They live on the road between the worlds. Not quite here. Not quite there. In between. Messengers between us and God. Between us and life on the other side. Very close to the edge.

The light and warmth of the sun grow weaker as we move toward the Solstice. Just as the sun holds in its leaving the promise to return, so you hold in your belly the promise that your father will live on in his children and grandchildren, in the memory of the people who knew him and loved him, and in the heart of God.

Blessings on you. And know that as you weep and mourn, as you hope and wait, the God who is like a mother and a father to us all weeps and waits with you.

Note: This piece was written for a friend who spent Advent this year knowing her father was dying and waiting for her child to be born.

Volume 15, Number 5, December 1993

Heresy

I have been rushing around inside my feminist theological brain for the last few months trying to keep up with the onslaught against women disguised as critiques of the Re-Imagining conference, held last November in Minneapolis. I finally stopped and said out loud to myself, "OK, which issue do you people want to talk about?" So far, I have read or heard comment on these: Imago Dei, atonement, suffering, Sophia, Biblical authority, milk and honey ritual, inclusive language, violence against women, lesbians, and giving thanks for women's sexuality. Someone is liable to throw abortion in here soon.

It is open season on feminist theology and on women. In a widely-circulated article about the Re-Imagining conference, Elizabeth Dodson Gray identifies the real issues as Power and Naming. The men can't stand it that a whole bunch of women got together to talk about the holy and did not ask for their response. Move over, buddy. We are here now, and even though you treat us badly, we are going to keep saying what we have to say.

And what is it that we have to say? That Christianity to date has been self-serving for men. That males created God in their own image. That Mary was not a virgin, that there were not just twelve disciples and they were not all men, that Mary Magdalene was not a prostitute but a leader in the early church who lost power to Peter and was then marginalized.

The part of me that has the personality of a lawyer sort of enjoys this fight. I stayed up until 2:00 in the morning recently reading theories of atonement and suffering. It was good for my brain. Atonement theories can seem a little ridiculous. God sent God's only child to earth and then sacrificed him on a cross so that God could love us? What? Jesus saved us. From what? The wrath of God who created us? I believe that Jesus was a Jewish reformer who was politically dangerous and was killed by the Romans through their puppet Jewish government. Jesus' followers were devastated by his death. The story of the resurrection may have been spin control. The church is the body of Christ, the resurrected body of Christ.

The Re-Imagining conference and feminists along with it are accused of heresy, blasphemy, and paganism. The dictionary says heresy is opinion contrary to the accepted religious opinions. If that is so, then what we are saying is heresy. So was the Protestant Reformation. Blasphemy is taking on the characteristics of God for yourself. No, feminist theology is not blasphemy. Blasphemy is what we have been living with for centuries: males taking on the characteristics of God for themselves. What we are trying to do now is to correct blasphemy. As for paganism, I would like people to know that there is a legitimate, respectable movement of paganism in this country that would probably be insulted to have the worship at the Re-Imagining conference called paganism.

A word about Sophia. A paper by the Presbyterian Coordinator for Theology and Worship said that the problem with the use of Sophia was that it did not conform to the Reformed trinitarian formulation for God. Neither does "Rock of my Salvation," but we use that language all the time and people don't start screaming about rock worship. I am not personally devoted to the trinitarian ascription for God. One of the things that we have been pushing for is expanding our images of God. When I ask other women how they imagine God, I hear lots of formulations outside of God the Father, Son and Holy Spirit, and outside Creator, Redeemer, and Sustainer. The use of Sophia was an attempt to try something new but something Biblical. It always surprises me that so many people get so upset when we replace male language for God with female language. It reminds me that they really must believe that God is male.

I have read rather poor attempts to criticize the milk and honey ritual for being a substitute for the Lord's Supper. Every invitation to a feast will sound like the words of institution. They all sound like being called in for supper. Can we have no other rituals at all? What about the Moravian Love Feast? Is that also heretical? The problem is how to make safe spaces for exploring new rituals without being reprimanded.

There is talk that churches will withhold money from the Presbyterian General Assembly and from presbyteries. That prompted one Presbyterian editor to write that a knife had been plunged into an already ill Presbyterian church. I did not know that the church was so ill, or that one ecumenical feminist conference could wound it. Why would someone choose to pronounce the church as ill, anyway? Is your local church ill? Is it ill because membership numbers have fallen, because dollars are down, because we have reorganized and reorganized and reorganized until no one can find anyone anymore? This conflict could be a sign of health. If the church is so split open by this debate, then these may be issues of real disagreement.

Why do some people try to stop the debate with an appeal to the peace and unity of the church? Sounds like power and control to me. Do they think we are going to blow ourselves to pieces? Conversely, why would *The Layman* (an unauthorized conservative Presbyterian publication) want to keep talking about these issues? Such debate may have a liberalizing influence in the long run. Some day we may thank *The Layman* and the *Good News* folks in the United Methodist Church for the publicity and for raising feminist theology to the level of national debate.

Most days I don't really care what these church commentators say. They can vote their votes and issue their papers. The church is changing. While some may try to stop it and others may try to push it faster, change is all around us. Women are leaders and preachers. Many churches use inclusive language for people if not for God. The new Methodist worship book even includes a liturgy for healing from miscarriage. It may be slow, but I do believe that in the last twenty years, we have changed the landscape of religion in America. It is amazing what throwing a little fertilizer around will do.

Note: A good resource on Sophia is Wisdom's Feast: Sophia in Study and Celebration *by Cady, Ronan, & Taussig (Harper & Row, 1989). For "divine child abuse" see* Christianity, Patriarchy and Abuse: A Feminist Critique *by Brown & Bohn (Pilgrim, 1989).*

Volume 16, Number 1, April 1994

Christian Feminism

Being a Christian feminist means understanding oppression through my own experience as a female and being in solidarity with all people who struggle for liberation.

I've been a feminist for over twenty years. My journey began in college, reading studies about differences in behavior and language between men and women. The only conversion experience I have ever had was on the quadrangle at the men's college where I spent my senior year. On a bright fall afternoon I saw the light, noticed and valued women, and became a feminist.

My journey with Christian feminism began in York Chapel exactly twenty years ago, when the second Interseminary Women's Conference was held at Duke Divinity School. I was not yet enrolled as a student, but I attended some of the program. I was twenty-three years old. As I sat and listened to Letty Russell and Sarah Bentley talk about women's roles in the church and society, something changed inside me forever.

When I entered the Divinity School in the fall of 1974, it was the same semester that the Duke Divinity School Women's Center opened its doors. I was riding the crest of a feminist wave.

I remember a small group of women would meet in the education lab in the basement of the new wing of the Divinity School. Sitting on the carpeted floor we risked saying out loud the images that each of us had for God: roaring wind, mother's arms, mystery, presence. There was no road ahead. We were making it up as we went.

I remember the first time I read Nelle Morton's essay in *Sexist Religion and Women in the Church* (Association, 1974). Nelle Morton suggested that God was a great ear, not just a great mouth in the sky, and that when we listen to each other we hear each other into speech.

I remember reading Letty Russell's *Human Liberation in a Feminist Perspective* (Westminster, 1974), in which she says there can be no servanthood for women until there is sisterhood, because the kind of service required of women in homes and churches—cooking and cleaning—is not a free choice but a kind of indentured servanthood or slavery.

As the years went along, I was grateful for the assistance of the Inclusive Language Lectionary so that I did not have to adjust all the unnecessarily masculine language in scripture in the middle of reading it aloud in churches. I was grateful for the new words to old hymns that carried more inclusive language and theology that I could believe.

I appreciated the work of Hebrew scholar Phyllis Trible on Genesis that helped me read the stories of the Creation and Fall in a new light and the work of Elisabeth Schüssler Fiorenza who, by employing a heuristic hermeneutic, finally was able to say that passages in the New Testament that are harmful to women should not be considered central to the word of God.

I watched and celebrated as increasing numbers of women became Presbyterian, United Methodist, and United Church of Christ ministers. Episcopal women were finally ordained. The original ones suffered greatly during and after the struggle for ordination. I celebrated as women became district superintendents and bishops, executive presbyters, and a woman became the General Secretary of the National Council of Churches.

And still the poor in this country are mostly women and their children. Violence against women and children continues in epidemic proportions. Women are sexually harassed in the workplace, on college campuses, and even in Divinity School classrooms.

So what is Christian feminism? For me it is a way of being in the church and in the world. It is a way of employing a hermeneutic of suspicion, of being suspicious. It is knowing that nearly every shred of our tradition was created by, translated by, or interpreted to me by men who neither shared my experience of being female nor held it in very high regard. On the contrary, from St. Augustine to Karl Barth, women have been held in very low regard, as second-class citizens in the church.

Being a Christian feminist means standing squarely in the middle of the church and saying that the image of God that we carry along in our tradition was created by males in the image of a powerful upper-class man.

Being a Christian feminist means holding up other images of God—as mother, lover, friend, presence, spirit, mystery—as alternatives to or additions to the patriarchal ones.

Being a Christian feminist also means facing the angry United Methodists and Presbyterians who seem to think that 2,200 women went to Minneapolis last November and Re-Imagined God into some sort of she-devil.

Being a Christian feminist means standing up against the onslaught of words, images, and actions which silence and diminish women.

And it means being concerned about men, that they be allowed to be whole people also, but not by putting women down.

Being a Christian feminist means understanding oppression through my own experience as a female and being in solidarity with all people who struggle for liberation.

Note: From a statement I made as part of a panel on Christian Feminism at Duke Divinity School, March 15, 1994.

Volume 16, Number 2, June 1994

Preaching

The phone rings at nine o'clock on a Saturday night. It is one of my women preacher friends. "I am never, ever, ever going to preach again. I hate it," she insists. We talk for over an hour. She is going to stay up most of the night worrying with her sermon anyway, so I don't feel guilty about cutting into her writing time. Together we try to figure out why she is so tortured by preaching. She is a great thinker and talker. I'd pay money to listen to her hold forth about almost anything for twenty minutes.

Not all my women clergy friends hate to preach, but many suffer over it. Are women trying to get it perfect? Are women afraid of being authoritative? I wonder why this is so hard for women.

The Resource Center has recently published a pamphlet by Ginny Purvis-Smith, *Experiences of Women Who Preach: Beginning a Conversation*. I remember something Ginny and I have talked about many times in connection with her pamphlet: We, women, did not create this form. We did not invent preaching.

How did we get this form we use at eleven o'clock on Sunday morning, anyway? I dig through rusty fragments of church history in my brain and fill in the gaps with imagination.

Long ago people huddled together in a cave while a medicine man or woman did some kind of magic. (Think *Clan of the Cave Bear*.) Later rites were performed by a priest or priestess at a sacred site like Stonehenge. Gradually female leaders faded from the picture. When holy writings were recorded, the priest or rabbi read from the holy book. During the Reformation, reformers decided that the priests should not lead the people around like sheep anymore. People needed to learn to read the Bible for themselves. (Eventually that even included women.)

Not only did people need to read, they needed to understand what they were reading. Enter: the sermon. The way to be sure people understand the Bible is to read it out loud and deliver a lecture on the text. Whose idea was that? Sounds like a form adopted from a university. If truth and knowledge come in discrete packages, then they can be distributed or disseminated in a lecture or sermon.

Preaching became the delivery of discrete packages of God's truth to people. No wonder I find preaching suspect as a form. I do not think truth can be distributed in neat bundles like little packets of seed.

I have had a related correspondence/argument with a theologian at the Presbyterian headquarters in Louisville this year about whether the words seminary, disseminate, and seminal have anything to do with the gender bias in the language. I claim they do. We agree that the root of these three words is semen, which means seed. By usage, the word semen came to mean male ejaculate, but it is a misnomer. Men do not carry seeds around inside them and then spew them out like a grass-seed-spreader. (Pollen might be a better image for what they carry. Pollen has part of what is needed for fertilization.) Because we use semen as a term for this male body fluid, I argue that the male image bleeds over into the meaning of seminary, seminal, and disseminate. They are all from the same root. The male Presbyterian theologian I was arguing with disagrees. He admits gender bias in the language but says seminal and seminary are not part of it. My women friends see a connection.

It's like white. In this culture we use white for beige-skinned people from Europe and black for brown-skinned people from Africa. We also use white for good or pure and black for evil or dangerous. Consequently, we cannot sing, "Wash me white as snow," and say that there is no racial inference in it. EuroAmericans have appropriated white for themselves just like men have appropriated semen/seed for themselves.

To say that on Sunday morning a preacher disseminates the word of God immediately sounds like spewing the truth all over people. Buckshot also comes to mind. In Ginny's pamphlet she talks about Henry Ward Beecher's metaphor for preaching as taking aim and hitting the congregation, like shooting a squirrel. It is not an accident that shooting would be a metaphor for this form (preaching) that men invented. My friend who called on Saturday night said, "Yes, they want me to knock 'em dead. That's the problem. I don't want to knock 'em dead."

Another image my friend and I came up with that Saturday night is that most Presbyterian worship is like making love, badly. People just sit there and the minister is supposed to do it all. If church is good it is because the minister did it right. What ever happened to worship as the work of the people?

My friend has stopped preaching for now. She says it is a great relief. For myself, when I consider what I want in worship, I get an image of a few folks who gather in a circle, some candles, silence, music, and a few words. Words about our lives, our families, violence, the world and how to make it better. Our fears, our hopes, our faith.

Note: The pamphlet by Ginny Purvis-Smith, Experiences of Women Who Preach: Beginning a Conversation, *is available from the Resource Center.*

Volume 16, Number 3, August 1994

Reunion

My grandmother made me a minister, and she didn't even know it was an option.

My grandmother was a Files, May Files Wilkirson. Her grandfather was one of the first white settlers in what became Hill County, Texas (about fifty miles south of Dallas). She was the youngest of nine children. By the time I came along, her life seemed to be taken up with three things: taking care of her aging widowed sisters (brothers and brothers-in-law had all given out earlier), being in charge of everything at the Presbyterian church, and driving me around Files Valley while telling me about the family.

I was her first grandchild. My other five cousins lived in the same town with her, Grandview, Texas (population 1,000). Neither family history nor local geography seemed to fascinate them, probably because it was part of their daily life. But for weeks every summer, I was her captive and enchanted audience. I lived in a city (Tulsa, Oklahoma) and I thought that everything about the lives of my small-town cattle-ranching kin was fascinating. To this day, my idea of a good time is to ride around the pastures in my uncle's pickup to count the cows and see if any have fallen in a ditch.

I attended my first family reunion last summer. I was not going to miss the chance to be with seventy-five of my closest relatives. I was determined to go, even when it cut into a two-week vacation at the North Carolina beach. I had the feeling that I would learn something about myself that I needed to know. Little did I suspect that I would learn things I did not want to know.

"Your daughter is going to have a pointy chin," I said to the young man holding the baby at the reunion. He looked at me as though he could have lived his whole life without ever hearing that, and it would have been just fine. He had recently married into the family and had no idea what I was talking about, so I told him. "We all have them," I said as I turned my head sideways and pointed to my chin. I don't think he got it. I don't think pointy chins are a big deal to people who don't have them.

I kept mentioning chins until a cousin from Austin finally responded. "Of course," she said. "We have pointy chins, deep set eyes, and high foreheads." I knew I was not making it up. Finally someone who pays attention to the obvious. I could give it up, about the chins. But there was more.

My uncle Oscar Lee turned to me just before lunch and asked me to return thanks. I couldn't catch my breath, and I couldn't think. What to say? Food, thank God for the food. I said, "Let us pray," and then I left my body. I heard myself say, "Gracious God, we are grateful that you have brought us to this day. We are grateful for this family, for the reconciliation that took place this weekend in the Presbyterian Church, and for the food we are about to receive. Let it nourish our bodies so that we might go forth from this place and show forth the values that have been taught to us by your son Jesus Christ, by the Presbyterian Church and by the Files Family. Amen."

That was the stupidest prayer. Thanking God for the Presbyterians and for this family. The food was dead animals, for God's sake. I've been furious with the Presbyterian Church (U.S.A.) for years for the way they have dealt with gay men and lesbians and for their response to the Re-Imagining conference. I'm a Democrat, a feminist, and a vegetarian in the middle of a rich Texas Republican cattle-ranching family.

I wanted for the floor to open up and swallow me. Instead I ate my lunch, or rather picked the sliced meat out of my sandwich while my husband made attempts at conversation with the other "married-ins." I don't think anyone noticed my discomfort.

What I discovered in that mortifying moment was that I am one of them. Here I thought I had lived my own life, making my own choices, and all of a sudden I felt like my being a Presbyterian minister had been predestined. While I may mock my conservative Texas relatives, I hang onto this family for a huge part of my identity. As Carol Adams says, it would be easier to stop being a Christian than to stop being a Presbyterian. When I'm honest I have to admit that it is very important to me that I come from somewhere and that I know who my people are.

My grandmother did her job very well. She gave me a passionate connection to her family, to the Presbyterian church, and to Texas just as surely as she gave me her pointy Scots-Irish chin. I know what to do with my chin: hold it down when I'm having my picture taken. It is my attachment to the church that gives me fits.

Volume 16, Number 4, December 1994

Compost

I cleaned out my compost bins early one morning in June. Well, one of them, anyway. I have two bins made of narrow wooden slats, stacked up like a split rail fence, that sit side by side at the back of the garden.

I decided to clean them out because I wanted to use some of the dirt and because my freezer was full. I freeze my clean kitchen scraps, a trick I learned from my friend Sally in Boston. She does it to keep them from stinking up the trash until she can get to the dump on Saturdays. I do it because it is easier than making frequent trips to the compost bin. The freezing may also aid in decomposition, but I don't really care about that part.

Freezing scraps is not a value-neutral activity. It used to drive my husband crazy to open the freezer and see bags of frozen food scraps, so he left and moved to the other side of the country. I have to warn guests to watch out if they open the freezer. A falling bag of frozen broccoli stalks and carrot tops can do serious harm.

I'm a lazy gardener and a lazy composter. I throw leaves, grass clippings, and clean kitchen scraps in the bins. They have to be clean scraps with no oil on them, because I don't want any more of those little brown furry mouse-looking creatures living in the bins and scaring the fool out of me every time I go near them. If I would water and turn the compost the rotting would go faster, but that would require dragging the hose across the yard and using a pitchfork to turn the pile. Someone stole the pitchfork a while ago, along with the lawn mower, sprayer, and long-handled loppers. I replaced the loppers; my young neighbor Jackson cuts the grass; I don't think I'll buy a new fork.

I keep my garden small and simple. Some years I'm even too lazy to grow tomatoes. My highly successful gardener friend Meredith used to give me tomato seeds, which I wouldn't plant. Now she gives me seedlings. Some years I get them in the ground before they die. Last summer we had a long drought. I finally got a few scrawny tomatoes in the fall. It might be more trouble than it's worth. Tomatoes all come in around here at the same time anyway. Meredith's always look better, and the organic tomatoes from Chatham County taste better than mine.

I have more luck growing flowers. I prefer flowers that cannot fail, like purple coneflowers and cosmos. I'm after color I can take in the house and something that the three-year-old down the alley will notice when she walks by with her dad and the dog.

Though I'm lazy about gardening and composting, I am zealous about spreading the word. I gave one household in the neighborhood a wire compost bin to encourage them along. They finally started throwing stuff in it and sure enough, it turned into dirt. I just love it that months later banana peels and orange rinds become rich crumbly earth full of fat worms.

On that morning in June, squatting in the middle of my compost bin in my yellow rubber garden clogs, I thought to myself: Gardening isn't just about tomatoes and flowers. It's about life. It's about the whole messy process. Gardening is about falling in love with dirt.

Volume 19, Number 1, March 1998

Following

When I left the Resource Center three years ago, I took a sabbatical for several months. I needed some time to regroup. Even though I wasn't sure what to do with myself, it was hard not to fill up my time with being busy. One day I sat down in the big green chair in my living room and said to myself: I'm going to sit here until I actually feel like doing something. I resisted the impulse to get up and run the vacuum cleaner or balance my check book. I sat there for the longest time.

I was burned out. I was tired of marching myself around, checking things off a list, and accomplishing goals. I did not feel like doing much of anything. What I wanted was to be left alone.

I spent several months doing very little. I organized my days around eating, sleeping, walking, journaling, and napping. I tried to take Brenda Ueland's advice in *If You Want to Write* (Graywolf, 1987) to spend a couple of hours a day moodling, that is doing nothing, fooling around.

I followed my energy, made some art, and took some classes. I visited museums and galleries, rented a studio, and led a few retreats and classes on creativity and spirituality. I went to bookstores and wrote down the names of books. Eventually I published a book catalog called *Words & Spirit*. Financial support from my husband allowed me to move slowly through this period.

I took a class at the Painting Experience in San Francisco last year. I call it "don't think, just paint." The method is described in *Life, Paint & Passion* by Michell Cassou and Stewart Cubley (Putnam, 1995). The leaders provided an array of paints, paper, and brushes, but the only instructions were to paint. They assured us, "These brushes have all been to school. Just put paint on them. They know what to do." I was encouraged to follow the energy and notice when it stopped. Sometimes it stopped when very strong feelings were coming up inside of me.

This winter I discovered InterPlay, an experience that brings together improvisational dance, music, and storytelling. It combines the insights of dance, theology, and psychology to help participants live more fully. InterPlay began in California, but we have two trained leaders in Raleigh, Ginny Going and Tom Henderson. I've started dancing/playing with them. Recently in a class some of us were complaining that we were thinking too hard about the movements. One of the leaders said, "Just wait until the movement comes of its own. Wait until your body wants to move."

I'm trying to learn to let the energy lead me, to get lost in the process and let go of the outcome, to let the Spirit lead.

An artist friend of mine tells her students they have to "give themselves to the process." She says you need to love the process, to get completely absorbed in making art. I think that is the only way to make it fun. She says it is the only way the work will ever be any good.

What a paradox. The only way for the product (the outcome) to be any good is to forget about the product, to let go of the outcome.

To worry too much about where the process will take you is to miss both the journey and the destination.

Volume 19, Number 1, March 1998

Labyrinth

The first time I walked the labyrinth at Grace Cathedral in San Francisco in the spring of 1996, I fell in love with this form of walking meditation.

The labyrinth at Grace is a forty-foot-wide circle containing a winding path that leads from the outer edge to the center. The design comes from Chartres Cathedral in France where it was laid into the floor in the thirteenth century.

The labyrinth has no dead ends or tricks. By following the path, the walker is assured of reaching the center. The path is complicated enough to prevent the walker from knowing how far it is to the beginning or the end. The mind gives up wondering and the walking itself becomes the point.

It was noisy at Grace Cathedral the day of my first visit. Some repair work was going on. As I walked the carpeted path towards the center, I felt I was moving towards the middle of myself. When I reached the center, I sat down to meditate. I felt I was being blessed by the Creator and received into a sacred womb.

I heard a supportive voice saying, "You can do this. You know what you need to know. You do not have to have any more degrees or credentials. You can do this. You know how to teach this."

I sat a while feeling the warm love of a mother's arms. I did not want to leave. I did not want to leave myself. I liked it there. I liked the words, "You can do this." I felt reassured that I could come again.

I was so enamored of the labyrinth after my first experience that I set my sights on making one. To understand the pattern, I drew it on paper 36 inches across. I then decided to try a paper labyrinth at a retreat. I rolled out newsprint to cover a forty-foot-square floor and drew the labyrinth with pencils and magic markers. Except for crinkling a little, the paper worked well enough.

More than a year after my first experience with the labyrinth, I finally bought enough heavy canvas to make a forty-by-forty-foot one of my own. The bolt of fabric was bigger than I, and when I knocked it over the whole studio shook. It took my friends and me 180 person-hours to cut, sew, draw, and paint a replica of the Chartres labyrinth onto the canvas. It made its first public appearance at Duke Divinity School in mid-September 1997.

Walking the labyrinth can be a way of centering yourself. The serpentine path provides a metaphor for life's journey. Walking can be a time to open the heart, to experience the presence of the holy, to attend to life's questions.

I have found the labyrinth to be a useful tool in workshops and retreats. It takes thirty minutes to an hour for a person to walk the labyrinth. It takes a group of twenty to thirty people an hour to an hour and a half. It is good to have time for individual reflection and then time for people to share their experiences with the group. A three-hour workshop allows time for introduction, walking and reflection. A longer workshop can include several times for walking, guided meditation, simple art projects, and journaling.

Lauren Artress, who created the labyrinth at Grace Cathedral and has been teaching people around the country about it, has written a very helpful book: *Walking a Sacred Path: Rediscovering the Labyrinth as a Sacred Tool* (Riverhead, 1996).

Volume 19, Number 1, March 1998

Weeding

One Friday morning in early June, I rushed out to my garden to plant some zinnia and basil seeds before it was too late. By early June it is already summer in the South. The growing season is well underway. The irises, peonies, and pansies are past. Day lilies and purple cone-flowers are blooming.

Before I could plant, I had to do some digging and weeding. I should have done this months ago, but I didn't. If I worry about all the things I should have done, I'll make myself miserable. I've decided not to be miserable anymore.

I was lucky. Rain the day before had left the ground perfect for digging. The soil fell away from the roots of the grass, clover, and broadleaf weeds without too much banging and shaking. In no time at all (well, a couple of hours) I had a three-by-six-foot area cleared beside the purple coneflowers.

While I was crawling around under the perennials, I remembered something I read a couple of years ago. Nancy Goodwin of Montrose Garden in Hillsborough, North Carolina, said, "Weeding is gardening." I agree. It is only when I'm weeding that I get down close enough to the plants to really look at them and to think about what they might need.

This is the eighth summer I've worked this particular garden. John tilled it for me as a birthday present before we even moved into the house in 1991. He liked operating the tiller. He wanted to do it again each year after that, but I planted perennials and they didn't need to be tilled. He took to renting a jumbo outdoor vacuum cleaner to suck up the leaves in the fall instead. (It must be a guy thing.)

By now my garden is well established, if not well kept. The oregano is as big as a doghouse. I used to plant vegetables, but they did so poorly that I felt like a cruel, incompetent human being. I now prefer hardy plants that take care of themselves and come back each year on their own.

The plants multiply. I make a habit of letting flower stalks stand long after they have bloomed. I figure the birds like the seeds. Each year I find daisies and lamb's ear growing in surprising new places. I pull coreopsis out like weeds. There is just too much of everything.

In a well-established garden like mine, gardening is mostly about removing things, clearing out, making space so that what is there can breathe and grow. (I'm of the English school of gardening and like things growing close together, but the little darlings can strangle one another if you don't give them some help.)

I've decided that weeding, writing, and mid-life are alike. They are all about clearing out. Generating words on paper has never been the problem for me. It's editing. The hard work is making choices, deciding what to leave out. I always want to say everything I've ever thought in a short, 600-word essay.

Mid-life is also like that. By forty-seven years of age, I've got more ideas and interests than time. If I add things like running the vacuum cleaner around once every two weeks, there simply are not enough hours in the day. In order to enjoy life, or to do anything with appropriate attention, I have to pick and choose.

Weeding creates space and helps to condition the soil. Where the dirt is soft and well worked, weeding is easier. Weeds like to grow in these spots, but it is also easier to pull them out.

It is similar for the human heart. I've heard that songwriter Leonard Cohen once said that while there are many paths to wisdom, they all begin with a broken heart. It is the breaking of my heart that has opened it and softened it over time.

Well-worked soil will grow both weeds and flowers. A soft, open heart can bear both joy and sorrow. Sorrow does not get stuck so easily in a heart that is soft. Pain passes through a heart that is open. Wisdom and joy are able to grow there with ease.

Volume 19, Number 2, July 1998

France

My only regret about college is that I never took an art history class, and my college had a really terrific department. My interest in the labyrinth has led me into some remedial work in this area. This is what learning should be like anyway. You get interested in something and follow the thread.

Fortunately, someone with years of work in art and art history came to Durham in early February. Meinrad Craighead, an artist in Albuquerque, once a monastic, always an inspiration, brought images and insights with her to Duke University. For six hours she showed slides of images of the feminine divine. When it was over I felt like I had participated in an endurance test or a dance-a-thon.

I've read plenty of books on the feminine divine and looked at images of the goddess, but seeing so many of them at once made it possible for them to begin to interact in my imagination.

I was particularly attracted to images of Isis and the Virgin Mary. Meinrad pointed out that Egyptian statues of Isis, seated with Horus (her son/consort) on her lap, look very much like medieval images of Mary holding Jesus. I heard her say that one could see such statues of Isis in the Louvre in Paris and ones of Mary in the Musée de Cluny.

Another image of Mary that has stayed with me is a small statue that opens up like a cabinet. Inside are images of the Father God, Jesus, and the Holy Spirit. If Mary really is "the mother of God," then all of God could be inside of her. Meinrad said one could find a similar statue at the Musée de Cluny.

That was enough motivation. I had been wanting to go to France to see the labyrinth at Chartres. Now, with these powerful images in my mind, I bought a cheap winter plane ticket to Paris. Off I went, in mid-February, with two companions, to see these things for myself.

Paris! I had forgotten that human beings could create such a beautiful city. I had forgotten that the streets and the river and the buildings themselves cry out to be adored. I had forgotten what a physical pleasure it is to sit in a warm little cafe (even a smoky one) and look out at the light leaving the evening sky and how gorgeous a stream of traffic can be. I had forgotten how wide a heart can open in the presence of cold wind, the rushing water of the Seine under foot, the sparkling Eiffel Tower in the distance.

I fell madly in love with the place and with some forgotten part of myself. I went to Paris to help only one person, to find only one person, myself. I found a deep connection to myself, to the most beautiful city in the world, and to images of the feminine divine.

You need to know that my work with the labyrinth has seduced me into a romance with the thirteenth century. One of my Catholic friends says that as a kid the nuns convinced her it would have been better to have lived in the Middle Ages. Even as a graduate of a Protestant seminary, all I really knew was that the Middle Ages were in the big blank space between Constantine and the Reformation.

I made a canvas replica of the Chartres labyrinth two years ago. From there I got interested in medieval cathedrals. You can't understand cathedrals without reading some history, so I read much of Barbara Tuchman's *A Distant Mirror* (Knopf, 1978), a beautifully written, exhaustive history of the effects of plague on thirteenth-century France. Then I went to France.

It feels like I got off the plane in Paris and went straight to the Louvre and the Musée de Cluny. In reality there were twenty-four hours in there somewhere of a dull, jet-lagged stupor. I do recall falling asleep at about two o'clock in the afternoon as though I were dead drunk. (I've never been dead drunk, mind you.) When I finally came to my senses, and could stand again, I went straight to the museums.

There they were, the statues in Meinrad's slides. Statue after statue of Mary holding Jesus. In some of them mother is offering child her left breast. And there, at the Louvre, were statues of Isis offering Horus her left breast. Same pose! I have long imagined a distant connection between the goddess and the Virgin Mary. The distance narrows.

For some background on cathedrals, we visited Notre Dame and Sainte-Chapelle. At Sainte-Chapelle we had a very theatrical American guide who is a student of art history. Just a few blocks from Notre Dame, Sainte-Chapelle was built in the thirteenth century by the French king Louis IX (St. Louis) to house his new relics. It seems the king's subjects were making oaths on his relics and not keeping their promises. He decided he needed a better set of relics, and bought "the crown of thorns." It is said that he paid more for the crown itself than he did to build the church to house it. To heighten the drama, he dressed in white and walked barefooted from the north of France into Paris with the crown of thorns.

Sainte-Chapelle is a little jewel box of a building. When the sun shines through the windows, the inside lights up like a kaleidoscope. I've never seen a church with more windows and less solid wall space. By the thirteenth century, architects had figured out how to direct the weight of the roof to interior pillars and buttress the walls from the outside, so that part of the exterior walls could be made of glass. At Sainte-Chapelle the buttresses are vertical braces that lean against outside walls. (The buttresses at Notre Dame and at Chartres are "flying," huge open arches that extend from high on the outside wall to the ground outside the church.) This ingenious architecture made room for huge expanses of stained glass, all but replacing the frescos of earlier churches.

Louis IX had one of the windows in Sainte-Chapelle filled with images of the kings of ancient Israel, each one being crowned. I'm afraid I would have missed this question on a pop quiz, but the kings of Israel were not crowned. They were anointed. Louis' point was that he was king. He had the crown of thorns, he was a king just like the ancient kings, and, by God, people had better obey him.

With this good background, my companions and I took a trip on the train to Chartres.

Volume 20, Number 1, March 1999

Chartres

Gothic cathedrals were built to be as tall and thin as possible, reaching, pointing upward toward the divine. They were designed so that the holy would resonate within their very dimensions, like a gigantic tuning fork to the divine. The most successful example of this architectural style anywhere in the world is the cathedral at Chartres.

The cathedral was destroyed by fire in the late twelfth century and was rebuilt in about twenty-five years, being completed in 1220. It is unmistakable. It's the one with the two unmatched spires. Built in different periods of history, there was no attempt to make the spires match. One bears the moon at its zenith, the other the sun. Science, mathematics, the zodiac—all of these belonged to God and appear many times in the sculpture and stained glass of this building.

I finally got it (I'm sure they teach you this in Art History 101) that the same images appear over and over again in the art of the Middle Ages. Scenes from the Bible, a set of almost codified scenes, recur in the windows, on the doorways, in the carvings of the choir screen (the wall behind the high altar). The Immaculate Conception (that is when Mary, not Jesus, was conceived without sin), the Annunciation (the angel appeared to Mary), the Presentation in the Temple. The cathedral is like a book. It captures, in images instead of words, stories from Christian history, scripture, and tradition.

Chartres is a Notre Dame Cathedral, dedicated to "Our Lady," the Virgin Mary. Many of the Notre Dame cathedrals in Europe are located on ancient sites where a goddess was once worshipped. There are about 170 images of the Virgin at Chartres. Above the high altar rises a twenty-foot statue of the virgin ascending into heaven, being lifted up by angels. In front of it stands a crucifix that is maybe three feet high, making Jesus seem rather insignificant by comparison. Everywhere you look there are statues and stained glass pictures of Mary. There was no question in my mind that Mary was the main character at Chartres.

If you walked in the main west door of the cathedral centuries ago, before the place was filled with chairs, you would certainly have noticed the forty-two-foot-wide circular pattern that covers a huge section of the floor between the entrance and the transept (where the two arms of the building cross). It amazes me now that I and everyone I know missed the labyrinth until recently. I had been there in the early 1970s but did not notice anything below my knees.

It was very satisfying to see the actual stones of the labyrinth. Large light-colored stones, some of them two or three feet long, fit together like puzzle pieces to form the paths of the labyrinth, while dark, almost black ones make the lines between the paths. The stones are worn, showing their eight hundred years of age.

Much of the labyrinth was covered with wooden chairs, set up for tourists and for worship. I walked the path but it was more of a gymnastic than a meditative experience. Finally, I sat down in the center and laid my hands on the cold stone. I felt like I was in exactly the right place, as though an internal compass has been insistently pointing me to that spot for several years.

What moved me even more than the labyrinth was the crypt (the basement). I had read about the nearly two thousand-year-old well in the crypt. A late afternoon tour took us to see it. The passage of time is evident in this underground world. Roman walls here, eleventh-century paintings there. The well simply captured me. I wanted to stay beside it forever. Wells were often goddess sites for ancient people, as were groves of trees and circles of stone. I looked down into its thirty-meter depths, and wondered about the deities its builders worshipped there. I understand the deepest portion is square and was built by the Celts. Nearly everyone agrees the well was a sacred site long before the Romans or the Christians arrived.

Just a few steps from the well is a statue of the Virgin holding Jesus. It is a replacement for a much older statue of a female figure holding a child that was destroyed during the French Revolution. The original statue may have been as old as the well. When Christian missionaries arrived at the site they may have told the people they were worshipping a precursor of the Virgin. Perhaps there is a connection between the goddess and the Virgin. Perhaps there were some who continued to see the goddess and her offspring in the Christian images of Mary and Jesus. It is hard to know what really happened, but I like to believe that feminine images of the divine have been venerated at Chartres for two millennia or longer.

When I looked down into the well, I noticed there was nothing in it but air. A well is a big open space that leads to water. The center of the labyrinth is also empty. Two years ago, when my friends and I were painting our labyrinth and came to the center, I was filled with anticipation. I thought it would be a big deal to paint the outline of the central rose pattern. But when I flopped that three-by-six-foot section of the canvas up on the painting table, there was nothing to paint but a few lines in the corners. The center of our labyrinth is empty.

When I reached the center of the labyrinth at Chartres, I found it too was empty. Not just plain empty, but missing something. There is a huge round scarred place in the center where a metal plaque of Theseus and the Minotaur used to be. The scene would have reminded people in the Middle Ages of the struggle between God and the devil, good and evil, or Christ and death. The plaque was pulled out during the French Revolution. It occurred to me that the old story at the center of the labyrinth has now been opened up, making room for more images, including the feminine divine.

Walking the labyrinth often feels like walking into the middle of myself. If the labyrinth is understood as a path to the unconscious or to the spirit world, then walking the labyrinth can be walking towards one's own shadow, that part of the self that has been rejected or pushed away. It is not easy, and not always pleasant, to see ourselves. Some say that when we see God, we see ourselves more clearly. The center of the labyrinth can feel like an enclosed womb or like an open clearing. It is whatever we need it to be. What I find there are myself and the holy.

Open. Empty. Possibility. The divine.

Volume 20, Number 1, March 1999

Wheel

In March I attended a workshop in Asheville on the Great Medicine Wheel. I was reminded, once again, that everything runs in cycles—seasons, years, a love, a life. We welcome birth, spring, growth, and even harvest. But we shrink from the memory of our losses and the inevitability of the ones ahead. It is the cycle of losing and dying that we humans resist.

Recently I've come to believe that if you cannot feel your losses, you can't feel the joy either. For most of us, it is only after some tremendous calamity, death, or breakup that we begin to open to our own pain. I've taken to saying that the spirit can't do anything with us until our shell has been broken.

I attended Helen Whiting's memorial service on a recent Sunday afternoon. Helen was fifty-two and died of cancer. She was one of the owners of Regulator Bookshop in Durham. I'm only sorry I did not know her better. What an interesting person she was, like a well-crafted story. She had passions: cooking, bridge, knitting, mystery stories, and basketball. She had old, old friends. She had a community of which she was a much loved and integral part. She lost her father when she was very small, but came from a family that loved her very much.

Listening to this absolutely wonderful crowd of folks at the memorial service talk about how much they loved Helen and how much a part of their lives she was brought to mind all the people I've loved and lost. All the beings who have been in the center of my life and are now at some distance. Seeing their faces, remembering their names, brings tears to my eyes. My grandmother, my father, old lovers. Friends who live a thousand miles away. I'm reminded that is what love does. It breaks your heart. Pain is the price of admission to a rich life, to a life with heart. Don't hold back the pain. Don't push it away. Doing so will only make you old before your time.

Love breaks your heart. If you have a child and love her more than anything in the whole world, she will grow up and move on to have her own life. If you have work, a pet, a gift, or a love, eventually it (or you) will fade or die.

We've all known people who refuse to let their hearts break, who close off the past, push away the memory of things that did not go well. It takes more energy to stay closed up and walled off, so much energy that one is in danger of shriveling up from the effort.

All of life is a cycle. Things come together and things fall apart, as Pema Chodron reminds us. Live in the present. Breathe into the moment. Feel your feelings. Be grateful for all that has come to you. Live without hesitation. Have no regrets. Life will open to you and will bring you more—more love, more feelings, and more losses. That's the deal. If you want the good stuff, you have to take the hard parts, too.

Volume 20, Number 1, March 1999

Annie

Every afternoon for a whole week this fall, I'd say to myself, "Oh, goodie, I get to go home and be with Annie tonight." I was reading *Traveling Mercies: Some Thoughts on Faith* (Pantheon, 1999), Anne Lamott's latest collection of essays. Nearly everyone says the same thing about this book, "I didn't want it to end. I just wanted her to keep talking to me." Reading the book was almost like having her curled up on the sofa next to me drinking a cup of tea and chatting away.

Lamott writes about her life, her faith, and her crazy relationships. She tracks her spiritual development from her California childhood in a nonreligious home with a father she adored. As an adult, she let her spirituality go underground. This book is the story of finding it again, her life in a church in Marin County, and the link between her recovery from drinking and finding her place with God.

Her essays are like delicious moral tales. Wise and wacky, they often leave me thinking, "Well, if she can survive life, so can I." No matter how bad things get (and having her father die of cancer, being bulimic and alcoholic, having a baby without a partner, and then having her best friend die of cancer is pretty challenging), she finds hope, humor, wisdom, and compassion.

Her recovery from alcoholism led her to St. Andrew Presbyterian Church, a predominantly African American church across the street from her favorite flea market. She says it was just the right place to go when recovering from a hangover—the flea market, not the church. But the singing from the church drew her in and eventually she was sitting inside listening to the music and to God. Now she talks to God regularly, and in *Traveling Mercies* she lets us listen in.

I came to know Lamott's work by reading *Bird by Bird* (Anchor, 1995), her wonderful book on writing and life. The title comes from a time when her brother was in a panic about a report he had to write on birds. Their father, a writer, told the boy there was nothing to do but take it one bird at a time, bird by bird. Lamott's great advice comes from years of writing and teaching writing. She says to write really shitty first drafts. (Lamott writes really shitty first drafts, and if you don't believe it, she says to ask her editor.) She also says not to write about anything bigger than what you can see through a one-inch picture frame.

Learning to trust God is a constant theme in Lamott's writing. She is not pious, but has a deep, abiding faith and a strong sense of God's presence in her life. She leans on God and asks God for what she needs. In *Operating Instructions* (Pantheon, 1993), an earlier book, Lamott tells of a time when her son was a baby and she was really short on money. She told God that if she was going to be able to support this baby, God had better do something. In a day or two, the phone rang and she was offered a monthly gig with a national magazine that paid exactly what they needed.

Learning to accept ourselves is a recurring theme in *Traveling Mercies*. In "The Aunties" (a term of endearment Lamott assigns to her thighs), she describes trying to feel like a beautiful human being in her bathing suit on the beach in Mexico with teenage girls wandering around. "Finally, mercifully, a van came along and took us up the hill. The girls got off before me and walked toward their rooms. God—they had the most incredibly small butts. It made me want to kill myself. When I got to my room, I took a long, hot shower and then stood studying myself naked in the mirror. I looked like Divine. But then I thought about the poor aunties, how awful it must feel to have me judging them so harshly—the darling aunties!"

Annie Lamott is quirky. Even her hair, which she now wears in blond dreadlocks, is quirky. In the piece called "Sister," she remembers her long struggle with her curly hair. "I don't think you're supposed to devote so much of your prayer life to the desperate hope that there not be any weather." My favorite part of this essay is when Lamott remembers something her friend Pammy said shortly before she died. They were at Macy's. Pammy had lost all her hair and was in a wheelchair.

Annie was modeling a short dress. "But then I asked whether it made me look big in the hips, and Pammy said, as clear and kind as a woman can be, 'Annie? You don't have that kind of time.'"

In *Traveling Mercies*, she speaks of her relationships with men. In the essay "Dad," she talks about the pain of breaking up with a man she adored and says, "I understood that it was going to have to do once again with having tried to get a man to fill the hole that began in childhood and that my dad's death widened."

In an essay called "Mom," she says that forgiveness is giving up all hope of having had a different past. In "Forgiveness," she shares her attempt to actually forgive someone. Instead of starting with someone she'd been mad at for a long time, she decides to try to forgive a woman who shows up at her son's school "wearing latex bicycle shorts nearly every day, and I will tell you why: because she can." Pretty quickly she realizes she needs to worry less about forgiving the woman and more about how judgmental and insecure she is being.

Do yourself a favor, read *Traveling Mercies*. Let this brilliant, witty, insightful writer teach you about compassion and offer you support for the life of faith.

Volume 20, Number 3, December 1999

Mercy

On Thursday evening, November 18, 1999, Dawud Abdullah Muhammad (born David Junior Brown) held his young grandchild on his knee. At two o'clock Friday morning, the state of North Carolina, with the late-night permission of Governor James B. Hunt, executed Muhammad by lethal injection. There are serious questions about whether he even committed the murders of which he was convicted. He had been on death row for nineteen years. Now he is dead.

I spent some time in November getting friends and colleagues to call and write Jim Hunt about Dawud Abdullah Muhammad. We were not successful in changing the governor's mind. We are, however, getting more and more people of faith involved in trying to stop this barbaric form of punishment (more aptly called revenge).

In November, I went to Asheville, North Carolina, to hear Sr. Helen Prejean, author of *Dead Man Walking* (Random House, 1993). Six hundred people showed up at First Baptist Church for Sr. Helen's lecture, which was sponsored by Holy Ground and Western Carolinians for Criminal Justice. Nearly everyone I know in western North Carolina was there.

Sr. Helen was amazing. Funny, warm, and hospitable, she's a woman who likes people and has a good time. A passionate fireball, she speaks eloquently and offers many reasons to be against the death penalty.

Most of the civilized nations of the world have done away with capital punishment, leaving the United States in the company of nations we think of as thugs and bullies.

Some people argue that the death penalty is a deterrent. The North Carolina governor still does. The only person deterred from committing a crime is the person who is executed.

Our criminal justice system is not infallible. Since the 1970s, there have been at least eighty-three people sentenced to death in this country who were later found to be innocent. A couple of Northwestern University journalism students found enough evidence in a few weeks of investigation to prove the innocence of one person on death row.

The death penalty is still fairly arbitrary. There are people in prison who committed more violent murders and got lighter sentences than people on death row. Decisions about which crimes are horrendous enough to deserve the death penalty and which are not lack consistency.

The death penalty is always torture. Sr. Helen described the terror and the nightmares suffered by the first man she visited on death row.

Poverty and race are factors in the death penalty. Defendants who can afford good legal counsel usually find a way to avoid the death penalty.

Punishments have been meted out in this country according to race since the 1600s when black and white indentured servants were given different punishments for the same crime. For generations the courts sentenced people according to their race.

Sr. Helen helped me understand another way that race functions in capital cases. If the crime is black on white, resources for investigation and prosecution are more likely to be committed to the case. More effort is put into getting a conviction and the most severe punishment.

Then there is the whole history of lynching. Thousands of black males in the South were hanged without benefit of investigation or prosecution. Sometimes I think we still have the death penalty in this country just so we can kill a black man accused of a crime against a white woman.

I got interested in the death penalty because of my friends. In *Fierce Tenderness* (Crossroad, 1992), Mary Hunt points out the effect on our lives of having justice-seeking friends. Twenty years ago, I dated a lawyer who passionately opposed the death penalty. Then in 1984 when Velma Barfield was scheduled to be executed in North Carolina, I had a couple of friends who knew her well. One friend worked at the women's prison, the other ran a criminal justice program. Their relationships with Velma made the issue more real for me. I realized that the person about to be executed was a friend of my friends.

On the night Velma was executed, a crowd of us stood outside Central Prison in Raleigh from late in the evening until the execution took place in the wee hours of the morning. I remember the eerie sight of the ambulance that finally carried her body away. It was another case in which our governor, Jim Hunt, refused to commute a sentence. That's when my outrage at the governor began. (He's been the governor off and on for a couple of decades.)

I wouldn't call myself a particularly good criminal justice advocate. If I were, I'd work on alternatives to incarceration, fair sentencing, prison crowding, and victims' rights. The issue I seem to pay attention to is the death penalty. It is the one that grabs hold of me and won't let go.

When one friend said she wasn't sure she could take on the death penalty right now, I said we could take turns by working on different issues and organizing our friends when something needs to be done. None of us can do everything at once. "The frenzy of the activist neutralizes her work for peace," reads the Thomas Merton quote over my desk.

Right now, I live close enough to the state capital to drive over for the prayer services the night before an execution. I stay for part of the vigil that follows and go home. Other friends come at 11:00 p.m. and stay through the end. We take different pieces. We do what we can, what feels right to each one of us.

One of the saddest prayer services this fall was for Harvey Lee Green. Through a relationship with the staff of Pullen Memorial Baptist Church in Raleigh, Harvey had become a member of the church about a year before his execution. He corresponded with people in the church, including some of the youth. His letters were read aloud at the prayer service, his art work was displayed, and people spoke of the warm, kind man who had become their friend. A whole congregation was changed forever.

My position is that no one should ever be executed. I don't care what they have done. Not even Jack the Ripper. The death penalty makes us all killers. It is cold-blooded, calculated, state-sanctioned murder. It is carried out in my name, and I want it to stop.

I'm often reminded of the words of a Holly Near song that echo words from *Dead Man Walking*, "Why do we kill people who are killing people to show that killing people is wrong?"

For more information contact Lao Rubert at the Carolina Justice Policy Center, 919-682-1149 or RubertL@aol.com, or Steve Dear at People of Faith Against the Death Penalty, sdear@pfadp.org.

Volume 20, Number 3, December 1999

Support

My life does not look the way I imagined it would. I live in a nice house with a big front porch all by myself. I have no children and no spouse. When I look around at my friends and community, I notice that I have about all the friendship, companionship, and love that one person could hope for, but it's is not made up of relatives. (They are mostly in Oklahoma, Texas, and Georgia.) It's not organized around my church. It is not even organized around my beloved neighborhood with its tree-lined streets and 1920s bungalows. It's made up of a network of friends (mostly women but not exclusively) who like each other, pay attention to each other, check in on each other, and make time for each other.

Take Julia, for example. I ran errands for her one afternoon this fall. One of her smart friends organized a bunch of people to run errands and make food when Julia's baby was born. I began to think about how I am connected to Julia. I'm not related to her. She's a lot younger than I am. She lives in my neighborhood, but not on my block. We don't work for the same organization or go to the same church. We are friends, but not even the closest of friends. She is part of my community.

I belong to a number of groups. I'm in a couple of meditation groups and an art group. I'm on a committee of the North Carolina Council of Churches that I've been on for twenty years. The committee meetings feel like old home week. We say we would pay money to attend. I'm in a small support group of clergywomen. I work in a studio/office with five other women. We host a holiday tea each year in December. We like one another and our friends seem to like each other. It's a lovely gathering.

I just don't go to a lot of stiff meetings like I used to. Most of the meetings I attend are gatherings of some piece of my community.

I invited twelve women to come to my house the night before I got divorced in August. It was a Sunday night, August 22, 1999. I was not sure what I wanted them to do, I just knew I wanted them to be with me.

I found a divorce ritual in Rosemary Ruether's *WomenChurch* (Harper & Row, 1985). I pulled together some of my favorite readings. I got the storage box marked "wedding" out of the guest room closet. I gathered up my bouquet (nine years dry), a red sash that bound our hands together, two pink candles we held at the end of the ceremony, the bulletin, and our vows. I set these up on the hearth in front of the fireplace along with our ketubah (a large document with signatures of the guests), my favorite wedding picture, and the wedding photo album.

My women friends came to my house and brought food. We ate chips, salsa, and wonderful guacamole sitting in the living room. I lit one of the pink candles and asked Mary to take the other one away. I sat on a small wooden stool in front of the fireplace and began, without really knowing what I was going to do. I said a few words, read the readings I had picked out, read our vows, offered a brief commentary on them, and cried. I asked people to join me in parts of the ceremony from *WomenChurch*. The part I liked best was pouring a cup of juice into a potted plant to release the future of the marriage that would not be.

Lise sang "I Will," a Beatles song. Margie read something I liked from her wedding. Mary Cleary read a quote. B.J. gave me a crystal, Susanya a carving of a butterfly. Some people cried, especially one woman who wished she had done something like this for herself when she was divorced.

I felt a little awkward, getting all that attention and not really knowing what I was doing, but it was good to have friends around me. When I went to the courthouse on Monday morning, I was ready. I know God's presence, in part through the love, support, and presence of friends. I am amazed as the days go by that I get what I need.

I also keep books and quotes around to remind me that my life is OK, that I just need to keep going, and that I'll learn what I need to along the way. Among the quotes on my wall is this one by Susan Virginia Hull, a clergywoman and artist in South Carolina.

The first and the last hope of this work
is that we may find
the candor to compose an original life,
the generosity to love lavishly and still lose,
the foolishness to reach, to fail,
and to find that we have fallen
into the depth of God.

Also hanging on my wall are these words which I wrote to a friend in an e-mail message. She noticed them and sent them back to me.

With the breakup of my marriage I'm all done
with work and relationships in which I do not feel
supported and cherished. I'm going to give this way
of living a try for a while. If I find it does not work,
I can always go back to doing things I don't like.

Volume 20, Number 3, December 1999

Church

I keep thinking about a recent exchange with a friend and her question, "So how do you get around being frustrated by affiliation with an overall stodgy denomination?"

Church is what it is. I decided a long time ago to stop torturing myself over it. I have not given up hope of changing it, but I have given up suffering over it. I find support and spiritual community where I can.

As for the Presbyterians, I'm stuck with them and they are stuck with me. Being a Presbyterian is as inextricable for me as being from Oklahoma, having southern ancestors, or having gone to a women's college. I am a feminist by choice. I am a Presbyterian because I was born into the midst of them. I could become a Buddhist, and then I'd be a Presbyterian Buddhist. The way Presbyterians think is so ingrained in me that I don't know how I'd even begin to get it out. They are like family for me. Married people can get divorced, but when it comes to blood relatives, you can dislike them or move away from them, but it is very hard to get unrelated to them.

When I was first ordained I liked going to Presbytery meetings. It was fun watching the institution at work. Soon it came to look like a bunch of men doing what they usually do. I stopped enjoying it. Some important issues are hammered out in those settings, but I've lost my patience for it. Most of these meetings feel like one group of people trying to exert their will over another group of people.

It feels to me like the real work of the church goes on in much more subtle ways. In the women's movement, I learned that a lot of change takes place one person at a time. I attend a Presbyterian church in a college town. As an ordained clergyperson, I'm not allowed to actually join. The congregation decided a few years ago to become a More Light congregation, which means it is welcoming and affirming of gay and lesbian people. Together we work toward making the denomination more welcoming. In the meantime we try to be the change that we seek. Even so, this congregation is a somewhat uncomfortable spiritual home.

When my mother was growing up, she attended a small town church in Texas that was filled with her relatives, dozens of aunts, uncles, and cousins. When I was growing up in Tulsa, I went to church with a number of my school chums. Church, like school, felt like one of my homes. As an only child, I was very glad to be in any setting with other children.

As an adult, I've never been part of a church that felt like that kind of home. I know some people find such a place. Going to seminary may have ruined all that for me. Being a feminist may make it nearly impossible.

My local congregation is still important to me. Attending (irregularly) comforts me and reminds me there are other people of faith seeking both the holy and a just world. I like the rhythm of going to church, and I have fairly limited expectations of what it will provide. It is not the center of my life. I like the people but notice that few of them number among my closest friends. Of the twelve women who were with me the night before I was divorced, none of them participate in my congregation.

I guess I have to remember that institutions are rarely comfortable places for feminists. Local churches are conservative institutions. They preserve the past and pass on the traditions. That's what they know how to do.

There was a time when I was very interested in changing the church. Women have changed the church some. There are lots more women clergy in mainline denominations than there were thirty years ago. There are even women leading services in Catholic parishes. Some congregations use inclusive language. But the church, the local church and the national denomination, are not where my heart and soul are now. What happens on Sunday morning is no longer the centerpiece of my spiritual practice, my faith, or my community. My heart and soul are in the numerous small groups in which I participate, groups where we sit together in silence, speak of our lives and work, and honor the mysterious workings of forgiveness and grace.

In some ways, I make my own church. I have gatherings at my house. I attend events. I trust what I believe, hope, need, and want. I take support from people in other denominations, other faiths, other traditions. I like interfaith settings these days. I yearn for folks who understand that God works among us in a multitude of ways and is not all that concerned about institutional affiliations.

Volume 21, Number 1, March 2000

Flying

I performed with the InterPlay dance company, Off the Deep End, on Friday night, February 4, at the Church of Reconciliation in Chapel Hill. While I have danced with all the people in the company, it was the first time I had been in one of their performances. I had a great time.

I set up one piece. I walked out to center waving my hand over my head hollering, "My turn, my turn." I stopped, looked around, and said, "I'm an extrovert. They said I could go early in the show."

I told about reading Sam Keen's *Learning to Fly* (Broadway Books, 1999). Sam is a philosopher and theologian whom some will remember from an earlier book, *To a Dancing God* (Harper & Row, 1970). A few years ago, at the tender age of sixty-two, Sam took up the flying trapeze. He heard a local news anchor mention that the San Francisco School of Circus Arts was offering trapeze classes to lay people and signed up. He fell in love with flying and eventually bought his own trapeze rig. With the rig set up on his farm in Sonoma County, he formed the Sonoma Trapeze Troupe and a program he calls "Upward Bound."

Since we did not have a trapeze rig set up in the church, I told the audience I was going to demonstrate the next best thing.

I asked for help from my colleagues. Several men stood on the far side of the stage from me. I ran across the floor and hurled myself into the arms of a waiting catcher. I did it three times. The last time, the man who caught me swung me around and around. I felt like I was flying.

On Sam Keen's book jacket, Clarissa Pinkola Estés praises Sam Keen's work for guiding us to "freedom from stagnating fears which can be attained by leaping towards the strong and outstretched arms of one's deepest desires."

When I dance, I sometimes feel like I'm being met by the outstretched arms of the divine. When I paint, I feel it again. It is a feeling I'm trying to have more of in my life, launching myself in the direction of my deep desires, instead of always in the direction of what I think I "ought" to be doing. It scares me. It usually makes me feel like I'm being irresponsible.

During January when much of normal life was paralyzed by the big snow, I spent many afternoons painting with watercolors. Some of the time I felt like I was supposed to be doing something else. Most of the time I just enjoyed myself and painted a lot with blue, white, and silver in honor of the snow.

Sam Keen says he is becoming a connoisseur of fear. I like that. Instead of moving away from things that scare him, like a new trick on the trapeze, he moves toward it. He's careful, more or less, preparing before attempting something a little beyond his skill level.

Part of flying is learning to fall. In dancing I'm told that if someone I'm leaning against moves away, it is my responsibility to know how I'm going to get to the ground. Sam Keen says that fliers learn to fall to the net before they learn to fly. I don't like falling, in dancing or in life. It scares me. I seem to have done a lot of it in recent years. Falling out of a marriage, falling out of relationships, falling down on the job. I still don't like it, but now I do it without getting as banged up as I used to.

There are lots of things besides falling that scare me. I don't just mean the big things like death, violence, and running out of money, all of which scare the bejesus out of me. I mean the normal things, like being honest with a friend about my feelings, painting when I really want to paint, and spending more time by myself. I have opportunities every single day to run across my fears, to feel my fears, and to leap toward the outstretched arms of my deepest desires. I get to choose whether to run the vacuum cleaner or to paint. Oddly enough, the more I paint and dance, the happier I am, and then I either vacuum or stop caring so much about whether it gets done.

Volume 21, Number 1, March 2000

On Foot

I've always said that one of the things I like about my neighborhood in central Durham is that I can walk everywhere. But I don't. Being a thoroughly modern person, I go for a long walk every day around the nearby college campus and then drive six blocks to my office with the excuse that I have someplace else to go later. I drive half a mile to the grocery store because there would be too much to carry home.

Occasionally in the summer, neighbors and I walk to dinner or the ice cream shop. When I worked downtown, I'd walk to work only if my car was broken. It took all of twelve minutes. Most of the time I drive.

This January, I spent three weeks on foot. It all started when my car broke down in Charlotte, North Carolina, where I had gone for a funeral. I left Durham, picked up a friend part way, made several stops in Charlotte, and went to the funeral. When it was time to drive home, my car began to hesitate, cut off, and finally died at a stoplight right in front of Presbyterian Hospital.

I called AAA. At the dealership twelve miles out of town, a swarm of mechanics in matching outfits spent nearly an hour without solving the problem. At 6:00 p.m., the car was running, the mechanics could not reproduce the problem, and not wanting to be stuck in Charlotte, I risked the two-and-a-half-hour drive home. Except for my being a nervous wreck, everything went fine. That was Thursday, January 6.

The next morning I drove to a meeting. It happened again. When I tried to drive home, the car hesitated, died, and would not start again. This time AAA towed the car to my local mechanics. "Keep it as long as you need to!" I said. "Lady, we think your car is possessed. You'd better take it to the dealership," responded the mechanic a week later. That was January 14.

Over the weekend I managed to take the car to the dealership, twenty-five miles away in Raleigh. On Monday the dealership found and repaired the problem. A dirty electrical connection was reading "hot" when it was not. My car was ready at the end of the day.

Tuesday was the first storm of what quickly became "the Great Winter of 2000." School was canceled three and a half days that week. A break in the weather allowed me to get my car back on Friday, January 21. By then I had been on foot and at the mercy of colleagues for two weeks. I had already discovered that there were a lot of things I didn't really need to do and places I didn't need to go.

Then it hit. Three days later, January 24. The biggest snow in recorded history in this part of North Carolina. Fifteen to twenty inches in places, like in front of my garage door. School was canceled for more days. My whole neighborhood was on foot.

I was reminded that this is the way life was when our houses were built in the 1920s. Streetcars carried people downtown, and there was a lot of walking. Neighborhood grocery stores, like the one that now serves as my office, were located within walking distance of many homes.

As I walked for fun, work, and groceries for the next week, I noticed life in the street. People speaking to each other. Small groups standing on street corners chatting. A crowd gathered at the top of the best sledding hill. Thanks to a neighbor's Flexible Flyer, I even took a few runs down the hill myself.

It's a lot like the hurricane three years ago. Nature, once again, drew us out of our houses and into the street where relationships and community grow. We spend too much time in buildings and cars. I'm grateful for three weeks of life on foot and for being forced to be out in the world moving slowly, meeting people, having adventures, not getting much accomplished, and remembering that life can be simple and good.

Volume 21, Number 1, March 2000

Garden

I stopped this morning on the way from the house to the garage. Pocketbook in hand, briefcase on my shoulder. To look at the garden. I set the briefcase down and said to myself, I'll pull just a handful of weeds. Twenty minutes later, I had pulled a couple of grocery bags full of weeds and had broken off the remaining dead flower stalks from last year.

I feel like a terribly unreliable friend to my garden. I look out the back windows of the house and think to myself, "Why are you still blooming? I've let the wire grass grow up among the irises. I forget to fertilize. The sweet peas have been about to strangle everything for the last three years. I stay one step ahead of the ivy covering the whole thing and making it look like one of those kudzu forests you see along southern highways. Why are you still blooming?"

This morning instead of berating myself, I stopped to notice. The rose bush I planted five years ago that has pooped along, is blooming its apricot heads off. The irises seem not to be concerned at all about the wire grass at their feet and are stretching happily towards the sun.

The big summer flowers in the middle of the garden have huge green leaves on them. The butterfly bush that I pruned after the snow in January is doing fine. The peonies (embarrassingly surrounded by weeds) have huge buds that are about to burst.

I get it. The garden grows along happily without much attention from me. It grows on the basis of work done years ago. The tilling John did in 1991 before we even moved into the house. The planting I did in subsequent years. The years of gardening Libby did that produced healthy irises that she shared with me. Even the one morning of raking I did in January, dumping pecan leaves here and there in piles in the garden, even that helped.

It is like love, or God. I live in a constant panic that I'm not doing whatever I'm supposed to do to insure that there will be enough love in my life. I'm so afraid that I'll look up one day and all my friends will have forgotten me and I won't be loved.

It is like God. I can go off for eons and come back and God will still be there. God is always right there. Well, in the South, where the winters are mild and the spring rain is plentiful, a garden goes right on growing. All the glory in my garden this spring is based on work done seasons, or years, ago. That's true for most gardens. A garden is not something you can go out and buy in an afternoon. A friendship is not something you can make in a day. A spiritual practice is not something developed in a week. Love is not something you can go get. We only have these things in our lives because we attend to them over time. *And* because they are forgiving, our gardens, our friends, the earth, and God.

The flowers are there. All I have to do is cut them and bring them in the house. Love is there, all I have to do is accept it.

Volume 21, Number 2, June 2000

Tibet

I went to Washington, D.C., over the Fourth of July this year and wound up singing gospel songs with Bernice Johnson Reagon and standing eye to eye with the Dalai Lama. Let me explain.

My friend Rachael wanted to see the Dalai Lama, who was speaking on the Washington Mall as part of the Smithsonian Folk Life Festival. She convinced me to go along. We stayed with friends in the suburbs and rode the subway into the city on Sunday morning, July 2, to find the Dalai Lama seated high on a stage in the middle of the Mall, chanting Monlam Chenmo (the Great Prayer Festival) for a crowd of several thousand people. Rachael and I waded into the crowd and stumbled onto friends from the Buddhist community in Raleigh who had gotten up very early to get their spots near the front. We squeezed ourselves in.

I sat cross-legged on the ground in the sun for two hours, a spiritual experience all by itself. My sun hat, a long-sleeved shirt, and a slight breeze kept me from passing out. Meanwhile, the sixty-five-year-old Dalai Lama spoke in a simple compassionate way about issues like ecology, overpopulation, and the need for limits to growth. He was both endearing and inspiring. "Growth cannot go on forever. Too much consumption. Mother earth is showing warning." "How many rings can one person need?" he asked. "If you wear lots of rings on all your fingers, how funny you will look." Seeing monks and nuns in the front of the audience, he pointed to them and commented that they were doing their part for population control.

He said that when we have negative emotions, it hurts us. When we are happy, it helps all creation. He said children need to be loved by their parents or else they have a lot of negative emotions and are not kind. He said poverty is not practical. It makes people angry and violent.

At the end of his speech, I was glad to have seen the Dalai Lama and was ready for some air-conditioning. After a couple of hours in the

National Gallery with the Impressionists and Georgia O'Keeffe, I was cool enough to brave the Mall again.

The exhibition in D.C. was a first in many ways. It was the largest exhibit of Tibetan arts and crafts ever outside Tibet, Nepal, and India. It was the first time the Dalai Lama led the Great Prayer Festival in the West. For me it was the first time the experiences of half a world away came to life again. I had seen Tibetan craftspeople at work in Nepal when I visited there in 1973. As we wandered through the brightly colored Tibetan craft booths, everything seemed so familiar. I could almost smell the incense and spices of Katmandu as I watched Tibetans spin and weave, make paper, shape brass bells, and paint images of Buddha and Green Tara.

I admire handmade objects and am fascinated by people who make things. Nearly every bowl and cup in my house has a story to go with it. Some of the traditional Tibetan arts and crafts are in danger of dying out. Cultural disruption and refugee life have disrupted the system of apprenticeships. Worldwide interest in Tibet and its crafts may make it possible to train the next generation and keep the crafts alive.

In the last decade, the plight of the Tibetan people has gotten more attention, due in large part to the efforts of the Dalai Lama. Perhaps you know about Tibet. When the Chinese invaded Tibet in 1950, there were about six million Tibetans in the country. Over the years, the Chinese have killed hundreds of thousands and destroyed many religious sites. The Chinese government relocated Chinese people to Tibet, clamped down on religious practices, and imposed Chinese as the official language. (Sounds like a plan to wipe out Tibetan religion and culture they could have borrowed from European settlers in North America.) The Dalai Lama fled Tibet in 1959. Today 140,000 Tibetans live in exile.

Late in the afternoon, music drew us into a tent in the part of the exhibit dedicated to Washington, D.C., folk life. Bernice Johnson Reagon, of Sweet Honey in the Rock, was singing with her daughter Toshi. Rachael and I sat down next to three Tibetan women who now live in Brooklyn, New York. We sang civil rights songs like "We Shall

Not Be Moved" with Tibetans. As we sang the chorus of one song, "How long? How long?" I thought that's exactly what Tibetan people must be asking. How long until they can have their country back.

That was Sunday. On Monday we got up early and went back down to the Mall to a Tibetan prayer service. At the end of the service one of the organizers made a point of saying, "Be sure to come back at eleven o'clock." We took the hint and returned to discover that His Holiness was going to tour the crafts area. I planted myself near the wood carver, just behind a display table. The Dalai Lama eventually came to look at carved incense holders. He stood on the other side of the table, about six feet from me.

Later that afternoon, as we toured the Holocaust Museum, my experiences of the weekend began to fit together. Jews, African Americans, Tibetans, Palestinians, Native Americans, Japanese Americans, on and on the list goes. Peoples who were forcibly removed from their homes and lands. The ancient Hebrews asked, "How can we sing God's song in a foreign land?" The amazing thing is that in spite of gross inhumanity, some people do figure out how to sing and dance, weave and paint, even in a foreign land. To do so is to proclaim freedom until justice reigns.

Volume 21, Number 3, October 2000

Enough

The Sounds of Silence retreat that I led at the beach in December was very peaceful, until we got the weather report. Saturday night at dinner, someone handed me a weather advisory saying that a big snowstorm was headed for Raleigh and Durham. The women attending the retreat were either from that area or had to drive through that area to get home. Most of us decided to stay the night and leave after breakfast on Sunday, cutting the retreat a couple of hours short. B.J., Lucy, and I piled into Lucy's Jeep and drove home through a blizzard. Oh, my! It was both beautiful and scary. Lucy pointed out that her Jeep looks like it should be four-wheel drive, but it is not. I was not at all sure we should have been on the road and was very glad not to be the one driving. When we got as far west as Raleigh, there was no snow, so we went to the North Carolina Museum of Art to see the Ansel Adams exhibit (third time for me). Afterwards, when we got back in Lucy's Jeep, it wouldn't start. The battery was dead. AAA and Lucy's husband got us home to Durham. Not a bad day for a blizzard and a dead battery.

The following Tuesday my office mates and I worked all day to get ready for our annual tea. RCWMS shares a small building with three writers and a landscape designer. We invite clients and friends to tea each December. This year's party was in honor of the 100th birthday of our building, which was built in 1900 and known for many years as the Watts Street Grocery. Scores of people came to visit, drink tea, and eat cookies.

Ira and Frances Welch were the last grocers. He died a few years ago, but she still lives next door and owns the building. I bought groceries from the Welches when I was in divinity school in the 1970s. I lived in the neighborhood and often stopped at the store on the way home in the afternoon. I liked to buy the figs that neighbors grew and brought in and the sausages and preserves that Mrs. Welch made and sold. A large drawing of the store hangs in Mrs. Welch's house. She loaned us a drawing to show at our party and came to the tea. Her Watts Street Baptist Church pastor, Mel Williams, breezed through on his way home from a funeral. It pleased Mrs. Welch. "He's never been in here before," she teased.

I bought a Christmas tree that same week, the first week of December. I borrowed a friend's husband and son to help me get it into my house. It took four trips to the Methodist church in my neighborhood—one to pick it out, one to attempt to pick it up on a cold night when they closed early, one to pay for it, and another trip to actually haul it home. The old guys around the fire pit at the tree lot kept saying, "Nice to see you again," and "No, we won't charge you extra for keeping the tree."

I love working in a one hundred-year-old building where I used to buy groceries. I love living in a neighborhood where I can walk, where I see the same guys at the tree lot year after year, where I can talk with my landlady about the sausages she used to make and how picky the meat inspectors were. These feel like the strands of a life being woven together into a cloth that supports more than just me. Some of the kids who came to the tea this year were smearing brownies on the furniture four years at our first tea. This year their parents hardly worried about them as they played outside with a few teenagers in charge.

Where am I going with all this? *Dayenu*. It would have been enough. (Do you know this word from the Seder service? If God had only brought us out of Egypt, *dayenu*. If God had only led us to Mt. Sinai, *dayenu*. If God had only given us the Torah, *dayenu*.) If I had only had a weekend of silence, it would have been enough, but I also saw the sunset. If I had only seen the sunset reflecting peach and fuchsia in the tide pools on the beach, it would have been enough, but it also snowed. If we had only gotten home safely, it would have been enough, but we also got to see art. If only a few friends had showed up for tea, it would have been enough, but many came and they also bought my watercolor cards and books. If I only got to watch children grow up, it would be enough. But no, God provides all of this and more. Every now and then, I remember to stop and say thank you.

Volume 21, Number 4, December 2000

Sitting

I'm trying to encourage the part of my spiritual practice that is about being grateful for whatever life, God, and the universe send me. I got some help with this at the Meditation Retreat for Activists and Organizers that RCWMS sponsored in November.

Therese Fitzgerald and Leslie Rawls were kind and patient retreat leaders who shared with participants the gentle wisdom of Thich Nhat Hanh, a Buddhist teacher and peace activist from Vietnam. I learned to eat in silence and to chew each bite thirty times. I watched the sunset and the full moon rise and the sunrise. I wandered silently, peacefully, aimlessly on the beach with twenty-five other people. But what taught me the most about gratitude was my chair.

We spent a lot of time in sitting meditation at the retreat. Sitting meditation is simply meditating in a seated position. Some limber folks, including our two leaders, sat on cushions on the floor. I sat in a chair.

I had a lot of discomfort while sitting in my chair. The chair was too big for me, a common problem for people under 5'5". I tried putting blocks under my feet, but nothing worked. I was so uncomfortable that I kept thinking to myself, "I'm going to die in two seconds." Two seconds later I'd still be alive, so I'd think, "In two more seconds, I'm really going to die." I didn't die, I just continued to be irritated with the chair.

Staying with my chair turned out to be very useful. In the days that followed the retreat, I realized that my experience with the chair was like my experience with other difficult situations or feelings. I think to myself, "I *can't* stand this." But I do stand it. And if I stay with it, it shifts and sometimes eases.

The morning after I got home from the retreat, I woke up with a new thought. I realized that my discomfort with not having a family or a partner is just like my discomfort with sitting. It is just discomfort. The idea that everything would be perfect if I had the right chair is just like the idea that everything would be perfect if my husband had not left, or if some fabulous person had stepped right in to take his place.

For the three years I've been alone, I've been saying to myself, "Nothing is really wrong. You are fine. Everything is going to be OK." Don't misunderstand. I was not a good sport about the breakup of my marriage. There was plenty of screaming and crying. I gave in to the grief over and over. I have been telling myself that I'm OK, because I am. After the retreat I began to understand this on a deeper level. The things that feel like they are wrong are not necessarily wrong. My being alone is not the problem. How I feel about it is the problem.

I notice that everything I complain about has an up side, and nearly everything I adore has a down side. Those Buddhists! They know that. It's in the story of the Zen Master and the cows. A Zen Master was sitting by the side of the road with his students when a frantic farmer came along. "Have you seen my cows?" asked the farmer. "They have gotten away." "No," said the Zen master, and the farmer ran on down the road in search of his cows. Turning to his students, the Zen master said, "You lucky people. You have no cows."

This is a time of year to be thankful, to be grateful for cows and for no cows. A time to be grateful for light and for darkness, for being with others and for being alone.

I've been feeling a slight sense of dread about the holidays. This is actually a new sensation for me. One of my callings in life has been to help other people learn to enjoy Christmas (birthdays, too). I'll spend the holidays with wonderful friends. That's not the problem. I think the dread comes from not having a family, a partner, or even a healthy dose of denial to protect me this year. (Watch out for this meditation stuff. Seeing your life clearly is not always comfortable.)

The holidays have a way of serving up a lifetime of accumulated losses for many of us. When I feel sadness about the past, first I flinch and then I want to go numb. If I'm lucky, I remember that all I need to do is to open my heart to whatever is inside, to feel the sadness or loss. Some days I can even feel a little grateful for surviving and growing. Opening my heart to my own difficult feelings is a challenge. So was staying in my chair.

I found myself recently telling a friend (a woman who has just had a relationship fall apart) that the good thing about having a partner during the holidays is that it saves you from one thing: not having a partner. Since I've had partners for most of my adult life, I've felt safe around the holidays. Now that I'm on my own, the holidays make me nervous. I'm trying to learn that how I am does not depend on someone else. It is hard to hold this idea and to admit, at the same time, that I prefer to share my life with another adult. It's a koan, an unanswerable riddle. How do we appreciate what is and hold open the possibility of something different?

I get along better when I can keep it straight that whatever suffering I may experience around being alone is just discomfort. It is just like sitting and being uncomfortable. My idea that everything would be better if I were not alone *is only an idea*. When I remember that, I can stand it. And I begin to notice the good things about it. I have lots of quiet and I don't have to argue with anyone about how to put the lights on the Christmas tree. All I need to do is be here right now, live today as consciously as I can. If the chair is uncomfortable, I don't need to do anything about it. I can just try to accept it and see if I can find a way to be grateful for an uncomfortable chair. Or even for being alone.

Volume 21, Number 4, December 2000

Father

Before I even opened my eyes on the morning of February 28, I was greeted by a slight sense of dread. It was only a moment before I remembered it was the last day of February and recognized the feeling.

I don't have to remember the date; my body remembers it for me. My father died on the last day of February, twenty-five years ago. He was only fifty-eight years old. Elmer Malcolm Stokes, born June 13, 1917, died February 29, 1976. Three out of four years, we don't even have the twenty-ninth of February, so I've fixed on the last day of the month.

As I lay waking, I wondered what I might do to honor my father's memory and make room for whatever grief might surface. Last year I got out more pictures of him and put them around where I could see them. This year the last day of February was also Ash Wednesday. Getting ashes seemed like a good option.

My father's people were Baptists. One of my cousins just sent me a Bible Daddy gave his mother in 1948 for her sixtieth birthday. I think of it as my Baptist Bible. When my father married my mother, he became a Presbyterian, more or less. In his later years, he returned to the Baptist theology of his childhood. Spending time in a Baptist church was another option for the day.

Looking for pictures of my father in the library at Duke came to mind as another possibility. He spent his first two years of college at Duke and I had meant to go look at old yearbooks ever since I arrived in Durham in 1973.

Ashes, a Baptist church, and the Duke library felt like the right containers for my body, my soul, and the memory of my father on the anniversary of his death. That decided, I got out of bed.

Later that morning, I called the Duke University Alumni office. My father grew up in Savannah, Georgia. Not all cities had twelve grades in those days, and I was never sure when he graduated from high school. Duke had my father listed, class of 1938. I called Perkins, the main library at Duke, and discovered the yearbook, *The Chanticleer*, is available in the University Archives located in the library.

I went to Perkins Library at four o'clock in the afternoon to look for my father. I rode the elevator to the third floor, walked into the University Archives, and there they all were, years of neatly shelved yearbooks. The photos of the freshman class in the 1935 *Chanticleer* were tiny, fifty to a page. But there he was, smiling into the camera, looking so young. He was only seventeen. The 1936 yearbook has a larger class picture as well as a swim team picture in which he looks quite proud. The archivists brought me university directories and the 1930s file on the swim team, the Duke "Devil Fish" or "Mermen." (Can you imagine today's Duke fans rooting for anyone called a merman?) My father was a "fancy diver." They don't call it that anymore, either.

I have had a rough go of it with my father. He was a bright, warm, funny man, a doctor with a great sense of adventure. But he drank, left my mother when I was thirteen, and died when I was not quite twenty-five. It took me years to stop being nearly blinded by my fury. The gently sanding process of time has made it possible for me to feel the anger and finally realize that even though the story reads like a disaster, I loved him and he loved me.

I walked out of the Duke library onto the university quadrangle, bright with late afternoon light. The bells of the Chapel were sounding five o'clock. The university directories had listed my father's rooms in Kilgo and Craven Quads, so I walked the hundred yards to the other end of the main quad to look at the dorms and then made my way to the Chapel for an Ash Wednesday service.

As I sat at one end of a dark brown pew, I thought to myself that my father could have sat in the same place all those years ago. It felt as though some small piece of him might still be there. A small, bright, energetic, attractive young man from Georgia.

Duke University was barely ten years old when he entered in 1934. Trinity College, which became Duke University, was an old college, but the indenture that created the University and the Gothic main campus were new indeed.

I was standing in the Duke Divinity School Women's Center in 1976 the day my mother called to tell me my father had died. All these years later, it was right to spend some time at Duke remembering my father.

I went home that evening and returned a call to my next-door neighbor, Evelyn Barbee Wheless. I happened to ask her about her own college experience and she said she had gone to Duke for one year, her freshman year, as a member of the class of 1938. She was in my father's class. She said she would look him up in her annual. These bits of connection have been here all along, waiting until the time was right for me to discover them.

Later that evening I went to the Ash Wednesday service at Watts Street Baptist Church. (I've never been to two Ash Wednesday services on the same day before.) I heard the familiar language of the service, "Remember you are dust, and to dust you will return." This time, though, instead of feeling sad, I felt comforted. We all come out of the earth and we return to it at the end of our lives. That's where my father's body is now, deep in the ground.

I had such a good experience in the library and at the church services that I felt sweetly sad. I thought I had more than survived the day of remembering my father. Some nameless grace had offered me ways of being with myself and with his memory.

The following Sunday, I saw a friend at church with his ten-year-old daughter. It reminded me that when I was ten, I still had a father, not just in heaven (take that in all its possible meanings) but in my house. Somehow it made me really miss my dad. Lest I escape too easily, the feeling lasted for days, but not forever. For Christians it is the season of Lent. The lengthening of the days. The scars of winter begin to heal. I have survived another season of remembering the dead. Outside the riot of spring has begun. Joy and sorrow, always together. Life goes on.

Volume 22, Number 1, April 2001

Mother

Margie called at 9:30 a.m. on a Thursday in March to say that she and her husband Stan were in the car on the way to the doctor's office. Her contractions were five minutes apart. It had begun. Another child was about to be born into the world. I was the backup birth coach. Margie said she'd let me know when they were headed for the hospital.

When was it that humans stopped worshipping this most wondrous and mysterious thing of all—birth? Why did we turn from a reverence for the labor of childbirth and turn toward the labor of Wall Street? Why did we give up honoring fertility and turn toward history?

I've been reading a wonderful book, *Longing for Darkness: Tara and the Black Madonna* by China Galland (Viking, 1990). It has caused me to think a lot about Mary, the Virgin Mary (who, scholars tell us, was not a virgin). In this tale of her spiritual journey, Galland draws on her own Roman Catholic background and her experience as a wilderness writer. She moves through meditation at Green Gulch Zen Center near her home in northern California, recovery from alcoholism, trekking in Nepal, learning about Tara (a female deity in Tibetan Buddhism), interviewing the Dalai Lama, and visiting Black Madonnas in Europe and south Texas.

As I was reading this book, it occurred to me that in almost any other religion, Mary would have been a deity. She is, after all, called the mother of God, so why wouldn't she be divine? There is a medieval statue of Mary in the Museé de Cluny in Paris that suggests as much. The skirt of this small wooden statue opens up like a cabinet. Inside is an image of God the Father with Jesus. (The Holy Spirit used to be in there, too, but fell out.) When I first saw this striking image of Mary a couple of years ago, I realized that I had seen images of Mary with Jesus but never Mary with the Trinity. It made me notice again how male the Christian Trinity is.

I think of Western religious history as a journey away from the feminine divine. Many ancient religions focused on the seasons and cycles of the earth and included images of the divine mother. The God of Christianity and Judaism is a God of history, a God of the word, and a Father God. The focus is not on the earth and the miracle of birth, but on God's saving acts in human history. Some argue that progress was made when people stopped making fertility (food and children) the focus of religion and turned to politics and a life of the mind. It may be so, but in Western civilization it led eventually to a lack of respect for the earth and for women.

Take the Reformation as one step in this journey. In some ways, the Reformation was one of the best things that ever happened for women. Reformers turned away from images and icons and toward the Bible. They wanted for everyone to learn to read the Bible, which eventually led to the education of women. Sadly, as images and icons were eliminated, images of Mary, the last vestiges of the feminine divine in Christianity, were tossed out with the rest.

I find myself longing for more connections to the seasons and cycles of the earth, for more appreciation of women, and for images of the feminine divine in Protestant Christianity. I've spent twenty-five years adjusting liturgical language to make it more inclusive, using inclusive versions of the Bible, looking for hymns that include images of God other than father and warrior. The mighty acts of God in history are important. So are the wonders and mystery of spring and of birth.

If you want to read more about the history of patriarchy and religion, look at Gerda Lerner's *The Creation of Patriarchy* (Oxford, 1986), Merlin Stone's *When God Was a Woman* (HBJ, 1976), or Uta Ranke-Heinemann's *Putting Away Childish Things* (HarperSF, 1994).

Margie's labor went very well. At about three o'clock in the afternoon, little Emiko's head came out. I began to cry at the sheer joy of it. She was 6 lb., 8 oz. and perfectly gorgeous. Mother, father, and child are all well and happy.

There was much that was remarkable about watching this child come into the world. The modern hospital where she was born, the monitor that allowed us to hear her heartbeat while she was still in the womb, the presence and involvement of her father, and the female doctor. But the most remarkable thing of all was that one more human being had been born.

Volume 22, Number 1, April 2001

Italy

I had my sun hat in my hand and my walking shoes on. I was headed out for a stroll through the farm across the road when I noticed a man unloading bread from a truck parked in front of the restaurant next to Piombaia (the *agriturismo* where I was staying, just south of Montalcino, a beautiful Tuscan town south of Siena). I ran over to the man dusted with flour who was unloading bread. "*Pane?*" I asked, bread being the first Italian word a traveler should learn after "*Dov'è bagno?*" for where's the bathroom. "*Sì!*" What did I think he was unloading, elephants?

"*Vorrei del pane,*" I said, in too loud a voice in order to compensate for not really speaking the language. "I want some bread." "*Sì!*" again. So I ran back up to my room, grabbed thousands of lires (a couple of dollars) and bought the most beautiful loaf of bread I've ever held in my own hands. It was long and flat, like an oversized football with all the air let out. I served it to my travelling companions for lunch a few hours later, along with some pasta and a simple sauce.

That was the day I figured out that Italians eat a big meal in the middle of the day because by three o'clock in the afternoon, the bread tastes like yesterday's bread. It is the same with scones in England. They both have a very short half-life (the rate at which atoms deteriorate). Saltless Tuscan bread tastes like heaven when it is fresh and like cardboard by late afternoon. Not a problem. The inventive Tuscans have endless uses for yesterday's bread. Put it in the bottom of a bowl of soup. Soak it in water, squeeze it out, and put it in salad. Grill it and add a sauce. Make it into breadcrumbs.

Two weeks in Italy in early May. That's the present I gave myself for my fiftieth birthday. I don't know exactly why I picked Italy except that a friend had been there a dozen years ago and reported that there was nothing better than grilled bread (yesterday's bread, no doubt) with fresh tomatoes, garlic, and olive oil on top. Something about it spoke to me. I started a year ago saying to anyone who would listen that I wanted to go to Tuscany. I wanted to see the countryside.

Trips to Italy in my twenties had taken me to the mountains to ski, to Florence for a day, and to Rome. I don't really like cities. (I thought I would die during the ten months I lived surrounded by stone and concrete in Philadelphia in 1990.) They have great museums, but on this trip I realized that the art in museums had mostly been yanked out of churches, and I was just as happy to see religious art in religious settings.

I did have two days in Florence and loved sitting for a long stretch staring at Michelangelo's *David* and standing in front of Botticelli's *Primavera*. The David is just so unabashedly a western Renaissance man. (And I do mean man.) He is big, beautiful, powerful, able to kill giants with a single stone, making everyone else feel small. Real guys hardly ever stand still and let you look at them like that.

As for Botticelli, the *Primavera* (Allegory of Spring) helped me actually see the landscape once I got out of the city and into the middle of the rolling Tuscan countryside. Early May is prime wildflower season in Italy. My travelling companion B.J. kept saying, "I can't believe I'm not in a movie set." The fields of flowers and the roadsides were so beautiful it looked like someone from the North Carolina Department of Transportation Wildflower Program had gotten there before us.

It is hard to know how much of what one sees in Tuscany is planned. Tourism is, after all, a major industry. I've read that if you buy one of those beautiful old stone houses, you can't even add a window to it without getting permission from the authorities. So even if there is a wildflower commission, Botticelli's paintings suggest the flowers have been there for a long time. Wildflowers, such as red poppies, white daisies, and a purple cone named Melissa, litter the fields. Sometimes one flower goes into manic overproduction and covers a whole swooping hillside in yellow. Georgia O'Keeffe said she painted huge flowers to get people to see them. Nature accomplishes the same thing in the Tuscan landscape through sheer quantity.

I loved the countryside and its still functional towns and villages. I spent a week in Umbria, the state south and east of Tuscany, in a borrowed house, in a tiny fifteenth-century walled village with only ten inhabitants. The house belongs to the sister of an English friend and has the most wonderful backyard garden of roses, irises, and other flowers. I was completely happy sitting in the garden, letting the hose drip at the base of a bush and watching the light change, while the village cats napped on the stone patio or held down the cool dirt in a pot of hostas. When I visited cities (Siena, Castiglione del Lago, Città della Pieve, Orvieto, Lucca, or Milano), I enjoyed sitting in a cafe in the late afternoon watching the light on the western façade of a cathedral.

I went to Italy to sit in a garden, write in my journal, walk through the countryside, and eat bread. After I bought bread off the bread truck that day, I did go for a walk. Two months later, the cathedrals have all run together, but I still remember walking on the road above the farms, along the crest of a hill, with Mt. Amiata in the distance. As I admired the view and the meadows of flowers, it was hard to feel anything but bliss.

Volume 22, Number 2, July 2001

Churches

I grew up Presbyterian in a buff-colored brick church with clean walls and polished pews. The glass in the long windows was tinted yellow, and the only icon in the sanctuary was a cross behind the communion table. Imagine my surprise and delight at seeing the cathedrals of northern Italy this spring. If my home church is a nice southern lady, these Italian architectural specimens are elaborately dressed queens. They look like jewel boxes on the outside and inside are dripping with fresh flowers, adorned with paintings fit for the Uffizi, and lit by scores of candles. I loved it!

I sat many an afternoon watching the light shift on the western façade of a cathedral. Sometimes I went inside at the appointed hour for the Mass. On a rainy afternoon in Siena, I admired the magnificent striped façade of the Duomo (cathedral) and wandered inside. I was quite taken with the geometric designs of the inlaid floor and eventually sat down to rest in a small circular chapel on the right side of the nave. While I was resting, preparations began for a Mass. As older women in dark clothing filtered in, I decided to keep my seat. When several of them spoke to me in Italian, I thought I'd been admitted to some club.

Not being a Catholic, it was hard for me to know exactly what was happening. Luckily, I could recognize the names of the main characters: *Jesù, Santa Maria,* and *Dio* (Jesus, Mary, and God). I never quite got the name of the saint for whom the rosary was being said, but the faithful said "*Santa Maria, Madre del Dio,*" so many times that I learned to mouth the prayer. While I never deciphered all the words, it was quite wonderful to sit in a room full of people who were praying to the Mother of God.

I had originally been drawn to this particular chapel because I liked the painting over the altar. The beautiful Madonna with a golden crown captured my imagination. I might have stayed for the whole Mass, I had a prime seat, but the guys in black dresses running the show finally got to me. Here was a whole room of women (and a couple of men) praying to a being they were calling the Mother of God, being led by two old guys who seemed to have no sense of the irony of the situation. Why would they? So, while my fellow worshippers were still counting out "Santa Marias," I slipped out.

I much preferred the evening service B.J. and I happened upon at the Abbey of Sant'Antimo near Montalcino. It was early evening. We were wandering around in the car looking for our *agriturismo* (think B&B). I'm a good navigator and even when lost can usually figure out where lost is. We had made the wrong choice among the small roads that led out of Montalcino. We finally determined that we were headed in the right direction but were never going to reach our destination. To correct our mistake, we cut across some five miles on a dirt road, hoping to reach our lodgings before dark.

Rounding a corner, B.J. suddenly stopped the car. There, a quarter of a mile below us, lay what had to be a very old church or monastery. Pale yellow in the early evening light, the building beckoned to us. We agreed that we did not care where we were or what time it was, we were going to go see what it was.

Walking from the parking area to the Abbey of Sant'Antimo, one has a picture postcard view of the twelfth-century church. The apse (don't think I'm that smart about architecture—I have to look all these words up—the apse is the rounded end of a church where the altar is) with its three small chapels appeared to lean into and bolster the taller nave beyond. We found enormous open wooden doors. Inside, the simple interior was so dimly lit that I could barely read the instructional signs. It was dusk. Compline, the last office or service of the day, would start in half an hour. Risking the inconvenience of a late arrival at our *agriturismo*, we decided to stay.

We took seats in the back of the church near the dark wooden Madonna. Having no idea of proper etiquette in such situations, we sat very still, ready to leave politely if asked. Eventually half a dozen other souls drifted in and sat down nearby. Then seven or eight monks filed into the choir and began to sing.

I had noticed some years ago during an Anonymous Four concert in the Duke University Chapel that a large stone building such as the Abbey of Sant'Antimo can function like another voice in a cappella music. The monks were not the most technically perfect voices I've ever heard, one was rather old and creaky, but the venue was the very best. Those stone walls have been echoing notes of praise and petition for centuries. They could almost make music by themselves.

Compline was short, too short for my delighted ears. As it concluded, several of the monks walked to the back of the church. They sat on the simple wooden pews or knelt on the stone floor before the Madonna. There we remained, in the soft candlelight, for a few minutes. There, in the infinity of the present moment, we rested, brothers and sisters, silently reverent before the Mother of God.

Volume 22, Number 2, July 2001

Market

A farmers' market makes life worth living. That's what I say to myself when I get up on Saturday mornings in the summer. For years, a trip to the farmers' market required my driving to the next county to the Carrboro Farmers' Market, a large open-air Saturday market with crafts, breads, organic produce and hordes of people. The only trouble was that it wound up taking the whole morning. It was not a bad way to spend a morning, but it took time away from sitting, walking, writing, and painting on Saturdays.

Then about three years ago a farmers' market opened at the old Durham Athletic Park, made famous by the movie *Bull Durham*. There in the parking lot where Susan Sarandon kissed Tim Robbins are twenty-five booths of fresh produce, home-baked goods, flowers, photographs, and soap. Some Saturday mornings there is even music. The best part is that the market is only six blocks from my house. I can go and come back in an hour. Other people could do it in half an hour, but I like to talk to the farmers.

There's Lea Thompson who is the treasurer of Red House Presbyterian Church, a country church an hour north of Durham. We recognized one another from my having baptized some children at that church. Next to Lea is an Amish woman in a traditional long dress and cap who sells baked goods with plenty of sugar in them. In the next booth is the Hare Krishna farmer with his organic greens. I like to buy organic greens and flowers from Libby Outlaw, a remarkable body worker who has walked the labyrinth with me. When the young people who are part of SEEDS (an urban gardening project) are there, I buy produce from them. I'm thrilled that someone is turning abandoned lots and corners of schoolyards into gardens.

I take my sun hat, a handful of grocery bags, and about twenty dollars. I come home with real food and the feeling that life is good. I have a garden of my own, which I plant and tend absentmindedly. I have four little basil plants, so I'll buy basil at the farmers' market until mine gets big enough to eat. I grow flowers, but right now all I have is purple coneflowers (which are bright pink), so I buy purple and yellow flowers to fill out a bouquet.

My friend Perry is usually at the farmers' market when it opens. I find it reassuring to know I'll see people I recognize, along with outrageous lavender gladiolus and multicolored squash. It fills me with gratitude to know someone is carefully tending God's green earth.

When I was in Italy in May, B.J. and I went to the central market in Florence. It was just around the corner from our hotel in a big old boxy two-story building. In broken Italian, I traded for the most beautiful fresh pasta, the best pesto sauce I've ever eaten, red sauce, olives, cheese, unsalted Tuscan bread, olive oil, balsamic vinegar and salad greens. I got a kick out of figuring out how to say, "*Mezzo*," for half as much as the clerk was holding.

The wonderful thing about a local market is that it sells local goods. I am almost as delighted by the sight of homemade apple pies at the farmers' market in Durham as I was by wheels of Parmesan cheese and piles of fresh pasta in Florence. I'm just grateful that there are still people in the world who touch the earth and its harvest with loving hands and share the bounty with joy.

Volume 22, Number 2, July 2001

September 11

The images of collapsing buildings, falling bodies, and injured people in New York, Washington, and Pennsylvania were shocking and numbing. How could this happen here? I am used to wars and most terrorism being off-site, on foreign soil. That was before Tuesday morning.

While the images were horrific, the rhetoric that began almost immediately was even more frightening. A chorus of male voices, sounding in unison, calling for war and revenge. The message was clear, "We will get them. We will find out who did this and we will make them pay." The President, leaders of Congress, the military men, all.

As the government gathered clues and fingers began to point to one wealthy man in the Middle East, even I wanted to scream and run in his direction brandishing a sword. How dare you blow up innocent people? How dare you scare the wits out of people all over this country?

My overwhelming feeling is that I want to *do* something. We all want to *do* something. Red Cross blood donation centers are overflowing with people who want to help now, not next week, *now*. My e-mail in-box has been flooded with suggestions of how to talk with children, limiting exposure to violent images and talking with them about how they feel. I want to know what to do about adults, especially the ones who are talking about war.

I recognize this feeling, this frantic urgency. I had it four years ago when my marriage broke up. I wanted to *do* something. It is a helpless feeling, alternately angry and distraught. I discovered at the time that anger seeks a target. I was hurt. I wanted to strike back. But hurting the person who hurt me would gain nothing. Bombing the hell out of Afghanistan or Pakistan, while it might provide some momentary satisfaction, will gain us nothing.

In my own devastation four years ago I learned that the best thing to do was to gather people around me and to be still. To be quiet. And so I have been gathering with friends and strangers, in interfaith settings, as often as possible.

That Tuesday night I sat in a service of worship at First Presbyterian Church in Durham, a citywide service with Protestants, Catholics, Muslims, and Jews. I listened to the wisdom of Jesus, Buddha, Jeremiah, and Muhammad. Representatives from each of these faiths offered an expression of shock, hurt, anger, and hope. Each one prayed for peace.

It is not an easy task to bring together people of different traditions. I know because I've been working in interfaith settings for twenty-five years. Some of our words and practices offend one another. Too often Christian people speak of Jesus Christ as Lord and Savior in settings where not everyone understands Jesus as such. In the memorial service at the National Cathedral on Thursday, I thought Billy Graham did everything but an altar call. When he spoke of people gathered in houses of worship to pray and reflect on Tuesday's events, he used the word "churches." Mosques, temples, synagogues and sangas do not understand themselves as churches. We can't just add a few people of other faiths, stir, and call it an interfaith gathering. For any gathering to be interfaith, it needs to include a deep respect for all faiths represented.

When such respect is present, interfaith gatherings can provide comfort and hope. Violence is born of fear. Fear is fed by rampant fundamentalism that tries to wipe out difference. Hope lies in the direction of respecting one another, honoring the wisdom in different traditions, and wanting to understand rather than obliterate those with whom we disagree.

I see fear in the faces of my friends who are "different." Arab Americans are afraid of a backlash. Muslim Americans who are not Arabs are afraid of being blamed on account of their religion. Jewish Americans are afraid that the United States might distance itself from Israel. Many in the United States are afraid of losing some of our individual liberties in the name of catching terrorists.

I want the violence to stop. I don't know how to stop it. "We'll get 'em and we'll make 'em pay" only leads to more anger, more fury, and more violence. In the wake of this kind of calamity, being still is a place to start. We can help one another feel the anger and grief. We can pray for wisdom in these difficult and confusing times. We can resist the urge to make someone pay for this. No one can pay for this. What can anyone pay a mother or a sister or a friend for the loss of a life? More death will not pay for the lives that have already been lost.

If we want to do something, we can write, call or e-mail our elected officials in Washington, D.C. Contact George W. Bush, 202-456-1111, or The White House, 1600 Pennsylvania Ave., NW, Washington, D.C. 20500. Contact a representative, through http://www.house.gov/writerep/or call the Capitol switchboard: 202-224-3121.

We can also get to know our neighbors, people in our city or town who are different. People from other countries or faiths. We have much to learn from one another. Together we can find a way to share the world in which we live.

Volume 22, Number 3, September 2001

Cleaning

After the winter holidays and a big snow in the first week of January, normal life should have resumed on Monday, January 7. Instead of charging off to work, I found myself under the guestroom bed, cleaning out accumulated junk and vacuuming up years of dust bunnies. Among the stored treasures I found seven or eight framed items belonging to my former husband, who's been gone for four years. I resolved not to return the items to deep storage under the bed but to send them to him or give them away. When I contacted him, he said he wanted them, and would gladly pay the shipping. I wrapped the framed pieces in old towels, put them in the trunk of my car, and set off for the local pack-and-post.

A funny thing happened on the way to the mail shop. After a stop at the bank and one at the local drug store, I got back in my car, turned the key, and nothing happened. No cranking, no clicking, nothing. I tried again. Nothing. Dead. That's when I called AAA.

For the next hour I stood in the doorway of the drug store watching the parking lot fill and empty. The automatic sliding doors opened and closed. Cold air blew in. People came and went, most in a hurry. I was stuck. I called a few friends. One kind soul came with jumper cables and tried to start the car. No luck. We puzzled over how a fairly new battery could be so dead.

Another friend agreed to come and wait with me. She appeared with homemade pizza in hand. An angel, but still no tow truck. I called AAA again. The truck driver was a little lost. We got the directions straight and minutes later a big bruiser of a truck rolled into the parking lot. The driver hauled a huge portable battery charger out of his truck, hooked it up, said, "Crank it." The car started. He claimed it was the size of his battery starter. I had my doubts. I drove my car a few blocks to the neighborhood service station and parked it, with the framed items still in the trunk.

One could say that the energy of cleaning out was so strong that it killed my car. Or one could say that my starter was worn out, which it was, and needed to be replaced, which it did.

There is lots of room under the guestroom bed now. January was a good time for cleaning out and starting over. When I finally went back to work, I started cleaning out filing cabinets, reading through twenty-five years of RCWMS files and getting ready for our anniversary celebration on September 21. A year that began with cleaning out has become one of honoring all that has gone before.

Volume 23, Number 1, April 2002

Peace

It was hard to feel much joy this Passover and Easter season with the news from the Middle East. First we heard a suicide bomber blew up a seder in Israel, killing many people. Then each day there was another suicide bombing and more people died. Then Israeli tanks surrounded Arafat's compound in Ramallah.

I received e-mails from friends who are geographically or personally close to the situation, filled with grief and fear for Israeli and Palestinian friends and family. In one message, a man in Ramallah anticipated his own arrest simply for being a Palestinian male. He had seen many other men between the ages of fifteen and forty-five arrested in recent days. Robert Fisk of the *Independent*, a British newspaper, also reported such arrests.

In response, I have taken up one of my least favorite disciplines, reading the news. Here's what I've learned.

Israel has, at present, a religiously and politically conservative government that supports only Orthodox Judaism and continues to rule the Palestinians and occupy their land.

Forced off their land at the end of the Second World War when the state of Israel was formed, Palestinians have lived in anger and desperation for generations. The territories they were allotted have been occupied by Israelis since 1967. Palestinians have needed their own state for decades.

Suicide bombings have now disrupted life everywhere in Israel and the occupied territories. In the *New York Times* on Easter Sunday, Thomas Friedman said that suicide bombings must be defeated as a strategy or they will continue to be used around the world.

Israelis have a right to peace and freedom. Palestinians deserve the same. Nothing can happen until the suicide bombings and the Israeli military action stops.

Read what you can. Go on-line and search for Robert Fisk of the *Independent*, Thomas Friedman of the *New York Times*, and anything in *Tikkun* magazine. Then contact the president, your representative, and your senators. Pray for a solution to the violence.

There are no longer sides to take. Suicide bombings must stop. The occupation must end. People of faith around the world must speak up so that there might be a resurrection of peace, and injustice might finally pass out of this land.

Volume 23, Number 1, April 2002

Gossip

It all started in Wylie's hospital room in January, 1989. Wylie, a Presbyterian minister, had just had major surgery a day or two before. A couple of other clergywomen and I showed up at the same time to lend our support. The conversation turned to a minister in my presbytery of whom none of us was fond. Someone in the room referred to him as "a real sleaze." Looking puzzled, another woman said, "You can't possibly know the story I know." Then another said, "You can't possibly know the story I know." A pattern was emerging. Three of us had experienced or heard firsthand accounts of this man's inappropriate behavior with women.

By a year later, a group in the presbytery had begun the process of filing a complaint against this man, having collected condemning stories that represented twenty women across twenty years. It had all begun with gossip.

As a child, I was told it was bad to talk about other people. I still think it impolite and try not to talk about people behind their backs. I have also come to see this social norm as one that can certainly be used by people with more power to keep people with less power from getting organized. Over time, silencing the talk or communication among women, workers, or slaves has limited their ability to act as a group. African drums were silenced on southern plantations to impede such communication. Gossip among women is condemned as idle. Some workplaces prohibit conversation about salary, your own or anyone else's. Women in academia and in the church would never have been able to lobby for better salaries had they not been able to talk to one another.

In *The Women's Encyclopedia of Myths and Secrets* (Harper & Row, 1983), Barbara Walker says that a gossip is "an archaic word for a woman." The original word was *godsib*, "one related to the gods," i.e., godmother. Queen Elizabeth I was the *gossip* at the baptism of her godson James VI of Scotland. According to Walker, a group of elder women were called *gossips* as a term of respect at first, after the peasant habit of calling older women "mother" or "grandmother." Modern usage arose from the conversation of *gossips,* hence "old wives' tales."

In *Open Secrets* (Doubleday, 2001), Richard Lischer's account of his first parish, there is a wonderful chapter on gossip. Lischer explains how this informal chain of communication worked in his small midwestern Lutheran church. Community opinions, acceptance, condemnation, and standards got worked out as small packets of information passed through the gossip mill. Though uncomfortable with the gossip, Lischer came to understand it as part as the way things are and as a rather effective form of grassroots theologizing.

Volume 23, Number 1, April 2002

Bowl

Here's what I do in the morning. I sit at my breakfast table, I eat yogurt and granola, and I write in my journal.

I've been eating breakfast out of the same light blue pottery bowls every morning for over twenty-five years. My friend Helen Crotwell took me to a kiln opening at Sue Anderson's sometime before I graduated from seminary in 1977. I bought a set of almost periwinkle bowls and mugs. I have other bowls, but I'm really only happy eating out of Sue's hand-turned bowls. I enjoy the slope of the sides and the ridges left by hands that shaped them years ago.

I use the same shaped spoon every day. I like the feel of it in my hand. When I travel, I notice that I really miss my bowl and spoon. I often take yogurt and granola with me when I travel, but it is never quite the same experience out of someone else's bowl.

Eating yogurt and granola out of a familiar bowl each morning pleases me. It soothes me. I don't have to work at figuring out what to eat. I don't have to think about it. It's like a hot cup of coffee, although I don't drink coffee. When I sit at my breakfast table, I'm comforted. I can relax.

Let me tell you about the table. I'm short, so tables and chairs are often a problem. My square wooden breakfast table sits beside the windows at the end of the kitchen. It has cross braces underneath, about eight inches off the floor, which are great for me. In order to write comfortably at the table, I have to put a pillow in the chair, but then my feet don't hit the floor. I put my feet on the cross braces and then I'm comfortable. For those of you who are taller than 5'1", this struggle with furniture may only be a faint memory from childhood. It is a constant problem in my life. Not being able to reach one's feet to the floor can cause tightness in the upper back and general crankiness. Having the table fit is as important as the bowl and spoon.

Nearly all of life is out of my control. But at least breakfast most mornings is not a surprise. In general I like improvisation. I keep my knees bent, ready for whatever comes. But it's really nice not to have to start making up my life or responding to the unexpected until *after* breakfast.

Maybe that's why some people drink coffee and read the newspaper. At least caffeine and disaster are things you can count on. It's a practice, though not one I recommend.

A spiritual practice is something you return to day after day. It's a place where judgement can be suspended and one can accept oneself. It can be meditation, yoga, washing dishes, or even eating breakfast.

Volume 23, Number 1, April 2002

25 Years

Over the Fourth of July weekend, I went to the Festival for the Eno, an annual music and crafts festival in Durham. Lots of sun, sweat, food, fun, and entertainment. It gave me a chance to visit with friends who make pots, pictures, and papercuts, hardy souls who tend booths for three days come rain or hundred-degree weather.

This year at the festival, I felt especially grateful to a man named George Holt, whom I hardly know. George did two things for me. He started a local folklife festival over twenty years ago that grew into the Festival for the Eno, and he gave me information on how to start a nonprofit organization twenty-five years ago.

When I graduated from seminary in the spring of 1977, there were few resources for women entering professional ministry. While in school, I spent a year as the Director of the Women's Center at Duke Divinity School and I learned women in ministry faced challenging issues such as isolation and sexual harassment. I knew that many women graduating from seminary were headed for churches in small towns across the South where nurses and teachers were the only professional women people had ever known. I figured these women were going to need support.

With materials from George Holt, the enthusiastic support of Helen Crotwell who was Associate Minister to Duke University, and the encouragement of seminary friends, I decided to start some kind of center. I thought that if I stood still and announced my intention to the world that people would find me. I imagined standing in a crowd holding a sign in the air that said, "Women and Ministry" or "Feminism and Religion."

That's sort of what I did. The sign said, "The Resource Center for Women and Ministry in the South, Inc." Never give anything a name that long. Only the most persistent have ever been able to remember it.

It did describe what we were up to, at least at first: resources, support, networking around women's issues, ministry, and social justice.

As time passed, Protestant denominations provided more resources and gatherings for clergywomen, and RCWMS went on to be a more general-purpose continuing education and resource program on women, religion, social justice, and spirituality.

Instead of holding a sign in the air or creating a web site (it was years before the World Wide Web), we started a newsletter to let people know what we were doing. I puzzled for months over a name for the newsletter. One day while out for a walk in my Greensboro neighborhood, it came to me. As I was crossing Elm Street, the name *South of the Garden* popped into my head. It's a play on the title of a feminist song by Dorie Elzey, "Out of the Garden." In the banner on the front of the newsletter, the "S" and the "h" in "South" are lighter in color and fade away. "South" becomes "out." The first issue of *South of the Garden* was published a year later, in October 1978.

I hardly ever felt like I knew what I was doing. I remember telling Tom Langford, then Dean of Duke Divinity School, about the nonprofit I was starting. "Very risky," he said. Risky? It just seemed like the only thing there was for me to do. I guess I did risk some things: salary and pension come to mind. But I'd do it all over again.

For the first six years, I worked for free, getting paid as a part-time campus minister to support my RCWMS habit. When working for free lost its appeal, we started trying to raise money. We sent out fundraising letters and grant proposals and began charging more for our conferences and workshops.

There was never a three-to-five-year plan. We followed our noses and the interests of the people who showed up for programs. We sponsored fourteen conferences with feminist speakers such as Rosemary Ruether, Phyllis Trible, Carter Heyward, Katie Cannon, Mary Hunt and others. RCWMS joined the North Carolina Council of Churches Committee for Equal Rights in sponsoring eleven conferences on women, faith, and social justice issues, with themes centered around economic justice and violence against women and children.

I got pretty good at managing conferences for a hundred people. I thought I liked planning big events. It grew out of childhood birthday parties. Each year my mother and I would pick a theme for my birthday party. I'd make invitations and together we'd come up with food and games. The backwards birthday party was my favorite. The children wore their clothes backwards, came in the back door and ate cake before lunch. I'm still doing it. When I turned fifty in 2001, I reserved a gymnasium, hired a rock and roll band, and invited a crowd of friends to come dance with me.

Eventually I wore out on planning big conferences. The joy went out of the work. I came to feel like I was pushing a pea across the floor with my nose. So, on the last day of March 1995, I closed the door and said good-bye to RCWMS.

The Board hired other directors, continued to publish a newsletter and put on more conferences and workshops. I had a really good rest for several months, wrote and painted a lot, and then set about reinventing my work. It wasn't long before I realized I was recreating the work I had done for RCWMS. When the call came from the Board in the spring of 1997, saying that they wanted to make a transition and wondered if I was interested in being the director once more, I was rested and ready to try again. My hope was that RCWMS could focus more on spiritual practice.

September 1997 brought three big events in my life. I finished a forty-by-forty-foot canvas labyrinth, I returned to RCWMS as Executive Director, and my marriage broke up. The timing of these three events strikes me as meaningful but it is still beyond me to extract the meaning. Life just is what it is. We just keep showing up, not knowing what's going to happen, and expecting healing. Life is like the weather in North Carolina. If you don't like it, stick around, it'll change one way or another.

So, here I am, twenty-five years later, still tending to this garden I planted years ago. Nothing looks quite like it did when we began. The staff, office, board, and programs have all changed. The constant has been the newsletter, *South of the Garden*.

The essays also changed over time. I started showing up more and more as myself. They have become reflections on life as well as theology and politics. There's more of what feels shaky and uncertain, more of the everyday stuff of life.

It has been a remarkable journey. I have never been able to see more than six to twelve months into the future. We've rarely had much money in the bank and often had almost none. Year after year I've said if there are no more people and no support we'll stop. Each year there have been more people who want to weave together feminist perspectives and spiritual practice as they work for a more just world. There is no way to understand it except to say that the One Who Gives Us Life and Breath has held us greatly in her hands and has carried us this far.

Each day is a gift. We never know what tomorrow will bring. The days add up to months, the months to years, the plants in the garden grow larger and multiply. I am so grateful to have been a part of cultivating the Resource Center for Women and Ministry in the South. We are not alone. God is with us.

Volume 23, Number 2, July 2002

Copies of this book may be ordered from:
The Resource Center for Women and Ministry in the South, Inc.
1202 Watts Street
Durham, North Carolina 27701
919-683-1236
rcwmsnc@aol.com